There is nothing more difficult to take in hand, more perilous
to conduct, or more uncertain in its success, than to take
the lead in the introduction of a new order of things.

Machiavelli, *The Prince.*

KU-256-351

Advantages
of the Metric System

A J Ede

Published for the Metrication Board
London: Her Majesty's Stationery Office 1972

© *Crown copyright 1972*

Prepared by the Metrication Board and the
Central Office of Information

SBN 11 700183 X

Contents

iv

Figures

The Metrication Board gratefully acknowledges permission to publish

Figure 8:
The Institution of Mechanical Engineers and Engineering Sciences Data
Unit, London

Figure 10:
The Society of Aeronautical Weight Engineers, Los Angeles, USA

1
Introduction

Any proposal to introduce a major reform arouses our instinctive opposition. We refuse to consider it objectively because our minds are clouded by a primitive fear of the strange and unfamiliar. The effects of this reaction are not wholly detrimental; at least it deters us from chasing wildly after every novelty, and helps to preserve a degree of stability in our affairs. Those who put forward new ideas must be prepared to struggle against our inertia with long and patient argument. History shows that a really convincing case will eventually persuade us to change our minds.

The idea of the general adoption of the metric system in the United Kingdom has, in some quarters, produced just such an instinctive reaction. It has also provoked another attitude which is equally characteristic, and is revealed by the way in which the system is being referred to disparagingly as 'French', 'Continental' or simply 'foreign'. To approve it implies that our own system is inferior, and this is something our insular self-esteem finds distasteful.

This book shows how the metric system was developed, logically and methodically, by scientists, engineers, merchants and statesmen of many countries, including our own. It is then compared with our present system in a variety of contexts, and its advantages are considered objectively, particularly in its modern form, the International System.

1.1 Origin and development of the imperial system

To appreciate the extent to which we depend on measurement units, or 'weights and measures' as they are called in legal phraseology, we have only to consider for a moment how we should get on without them. The housewife needs to know how much milk or potatoes she is getting for her money, and she can only be told—and see for herself that she is not being deceived—if a recognised set of units is available, together with the means for measurement. The same is true throughout our society, and it is not too much to say that without standardised measurement units all manufacture and commerce would come to a halt. Our extensive vocabulary of words like large and small, fast and slow, heavy and light, is altogether too indefinite for any but the most casual communication.

In antiquity, the use of units seems to have developed at least as early as writing; crude measuring-rods were probably used many thousands of years earlier [1]. The Old Testament contains not merely straight-forward references to the use of the cubit, shekel and ephah, as in the dimensions of Noah's ark and the amount of flour or cinnamon required for an offering, but clear indications of a highly developed system in such remarks as 'shekels of the standard recognised by merchants' and 'there are twenty gerahs to a shekel' [2].

The collection of units now usually called 'imperial' is also of ancient origin, and its gradual evolution to the present form was governed by two basic requirements. In the days when arithmetic and the art of metrology were in their infancy, and their mysteries were understood by few, it was essential to be able to express the basic quantities of length, area, volume, and weight in their commonly occurring magnitudes, without the use of fractions or very large numbers, and to be able to measure these quantities simply and accurately.

Both of these requirements led to the proliferation of units of different sizes. The family of units for length, for example, comprised the barley-corn, inch, foot, yard, rod, furlong, mile and league, together with others added for particular applications, including the ell, fathom, chain and nautical mile. Practical considerations, such as the ease of making a volume measure in contrast to the difficulty of constructing an accurate weighing device (and of ensuring that it had not been tampered with), also had a considerable influence, and gave rise to yet more units: many different gallons, bushels and barrels came into use because it became customary for certain commodities to be measured only with their own special containers.

The gradual development of travel and trade led to a realisation that the primitive system had a number of serious defects. The first to be tackled was the considerable variation in different parts of the country between the sizes of common named units, such as the gallon. The second was the absence of simple ratios between different units for the same quantity, since they had been developed independently. From about AD 1000 onwards a great deal of effort was devoted by legislators to enforcing uniformity, adjusting the values of units to make the ratios between them into whole numbers, and defining units with as much precision as was then possible. From all this prolonged activity emerged our familiar collection of units.

As would be expected, it satisfies the basic requirements admirably. It does so, however, at the cost of an astonishing complexity. A typical technical handbook will reveal the existence of a multitude of units, inter-related by numbers which seem to have no rhyme or reason and can only be learned by heart. Perhaps we need not be too concerned with the clothworkers' nail ($2\frac{1}{4}$ in), the surveyors' link (7.92 in), or the fact that there are four different poles and three different chains; nor by the stack of hay (108 ft^3) or the cord of timber (128 ft^3); nor by old capacity measures like the anker, runlet, tierce, hogshead, puncheon, pipe, butt, tun, firkin, bag, coombe or chaldron; these are all specialised units, mostly obsolete or obsolescent, used only in very limited sections of commerce or industry. Almost everyone, however, has to be familiar with the following units and associated ratio numbers:

inch × 12	= foot
foot × 3	= yard
yard × 22	= chain
chain × 10	= furlong
furlong × 8	= mile

together with such composite numbers as 36, 220, 1760 and 5280;

square inch × 144	= square foot
square foot × 9	= square yard
square yard × 1210	= rood
rood × 4	= acre
acre × 640	= square mile

together with 4840;

cubic inch × 1728	= cubic foot
cubic foot × 27	= cubic yard;
fluid ounce × 5	= gill
gill × 4	= pint

3

$$\begin{array}{ll}
\text{pint} \times 2 & = \text{quart} \\
\text{quart} \times 4 & = \text{gallon;} \\
\text{ounce} \times 16 & = \text{pound} \\
\text{pound} \times 14 & = \text{stone} \\
\text{stone} \times 2 & = \text{quarter} \\
\text{quarter} \times 4 & = \text{hundredweight} \\
\text{hundredweight} \times 20 & = \text{ton}
\end{array}$$

together with 112 and 2240.

And we probably recall that 60 miles per hour equals 88 feet per second.

The outstanding characteristic of this system is the existence of a great many units, interrelated by a great many different numbers. The metric system deliberately attempts to avoid this feature without losing sight of the objectives which gave rise to it. To see whether its avoidance constitutes an advantage it is necessary to examine our system of numbers and arithmetic.

1.2 Decimal arithmetic

We use a decimal system, in that a special significance is attached to the number ten. We indicate numbers from one to nine by means of special symbols, but when we reach ten we start again and use a one, placing it, however, in a different position and adding a nought to avoid any misunderstanding. By this means we need only ten distinct symbols. When we multiply, say, eight by three, we note that the product may be regarded as consisting of two tens and four more, and we write 24. When we multiply 24 by 7 we operate first on the 4, noting that the product is 28; we write down the 8 and 'carry' two tens; we then operate on the 2 to get 14 (tens), add on the 2 we have 'carried' to get 16, and finally write down 168. In this way any multiplication, however large, is broken down into a series of elementary single-figure multiplications. Ignoring the special case where one number is zero or unity, only 36 different multiplications are possible, and these are well within our capacity to memorise. The 'multiplication tables', together with a few working rules, constitute our basic skill of arithmetic.

Consider now how we proceed when we have to deal with numbers less than one. The primitive attitude to such numbers is to see them as resulting from dividing a whole into a number of parts; three quarters, for instance; and we write $\frac{3}{4}$. Suppose we wish to multiply $3\frac{5}{16}$ by $15\frac{2}{3}$. We start by converting these expressions to 'improper' fractions greater than one: $16 \times 3 = 48$, $+5 = 53$, $\frac{53}{16}$; $3 \times 15 = 45$, $+2 = 47$, $\frac{47}{3}$. Then we note that $\frac{53}{16} \times \frac{47}{3} = \frac{53 \times 47}{16 \times 3}$, and carry out two multiplications, producing $\frac{2491}{48}$. This is not easily appreciated as it stands, so we divide by 48 to get the final answer, $51\frac{43}{48}$. Although this calculation has been based on the standard procedures of elementary arithmetic, it involves them in a much more complicated sequence. The mastery of such operations is one of the major obstacles the child at school has to surmount, and even when this has been successfully accomplished it still remains as a fact to be reckoned with that the manipulation of fractions is time-consuming and a source of error.

In the sixteenth century, mathematicians began to realise that a remarkable simplification results when fractions based on ten are used; tenths, hundredths, and so on. The following example is comparable with the one just considered: we wish to multiply $3\frac{3}{10}$ by $15\frac{7}{10}$. Using the same procedure, the conversion to improper fractions involves merely a rewriting as $\frac{33}{10} \times \frac{157}{10}$. A single multiplication produces $\frac{5181}{100}$, which may be rewritten at once as $51\frac{81}{100}$. The calculation has in effect been reduced to a single, straightforward whole-number multiplication.

It was quickly realised that, assuming one was prepared to work entirely in terms of 'decimal' fractions, there was no need to write down all the tens, and after a variety of methods had been tried out, opinion settled in favour of the now familiar decimal point. The above calculation then appeared as $3.3 \times 15.7 = 51.81$, and it will be seen that the procedure followed is almost identically the same as in evaluating 33×157. The complications introduced by fractions have entirely disappeared.

The relevance of this to the question of units can be seen from the following simple calculation. It is required to find the weight of a length of chain, 15 yards 2 feet long, given that the weight of one yard of chain is 3 pounds 5 ounces. This is a problem in what is known as 'compound arithmetic' and the first step is to reduce the number of units involved. If we put 15 yards 2 feet equals $15\frac{2}{3}$ yards, and 3 pounds 5 ounces equals $3\frac{5}{16}$ pounds, we are faced with evaluating $3\frac{5}{16} \times 15\frac{2}{3}$, and this is precisely the same calculation as the one just considered. There are other ways of proceeding but they lead essentially in the same direction. The use of units related by non-decimal numbers such as 3 and 16 leads directly to fractions and compound arithmetic and the difficulties associated with them. We are continually multiplying and dividing by numbers which are not an essential part of the calculations: they arise solely from the units we are using.

It took nearly a hundred years before it was realised that the full

5

advantages of the new decimal arithmetic could only be realised if weights and measures were also decimalised, ie if units in a series were related by tens only.

1.3 Origin of the metric system

The first well-defined proposal along these lines appears to have been made by the Abbé Mouton of Lyons in 1671, but it is interesting to note that as early as 1620 Edmund Gunter in this country had proposed a decimal measure for surveying, with a chain of 100 links. Sir Christopher Wren, among others, was interested in Mouton's ideas, but progress was very slow and in 1783, over a hundred years later, we still find James Watt campaigning about the desirability of a generally agreed decimalised system of units. It seems probable that he discussed the matter when, a little later, he met a group of people in Paris who were much interested in weights and measures generally. France was then in a state of intellectual ferment and in 1790, at the instigation of Talleyrand, a committee of experts (some of whom had been in touch with Watt) was formally constituted on behalf of the French Academy, and instructed to devise a new system of units; the outcome of its deliberations was the metric system.

In the same year Thomas Jefferson proposed a highly developed decimalised system in the USA, and it is fascinating to speculate on what might have been the consequence had it been adopted; but Congress was too busy with other matters and the opportunity was missed. In view of the interest known to exist in England, attempts were made to enlist our support for the new metric system, but by that time events had produced a wave of anti-French feeling and these overtures were ignored. The metric system, therefore, though international in origin, was forced to make its first steps in the world with support confined to those countries then under the influence of France.

The system recognised the need for units of different sizes, but set about producing them in a methodical manner. For each quantity, such as length or weight, a single, carefully defined unit was chosen as the starting-point, and other units for the same quantity were formed from it by successive multiplication or division by 10. The confusing multiplicity of names was avoided as far as possible by creating new names only for the primary units, and adding standard prefixes to form the related units. Thus having chosen the **metre** as unit of length and the **gramme** as unit of weight, the addition of the prefix 'kilo', meaning multiplied by 1000, produced the kilometre of 1000 metres and the

6

kilogramme of 1000 grammes. The other primary units in the original 1795 series were the **are** for area, the **litre** for volume, the **stere** for capacity (used chiefly for measuring firewood) and the **franc** for money. Prefixes representing factors from ten thousand to one thousandth were named.

The advantages of the primitive metric system may be summarised as follows:

1 It provided units of convenient size for virtually all measurements likely to be made.

2 The effort of memory required to master the whole system was small.

3 The system made it possible to use decimal arithmetic.

4 It offered a new flexibility in handling related units. (Consider a length quoted in imperial units as 5 yards, 2 feet, $3\frac{1}{4}$ inches. We can do nothing more with this without introducing some arithmetic. A corresponding metric measurement might appear as 5 metres, 3 decimetres, 7 centimetres, 4 millimetres; but it could equally well be written as 5.374 metres, 537.4 centimetres, or 5374 milli-metres, without any arithmetic at all.)

5 The availability of an entirely new, well-defined and superior system of units, at a time when international commerce was rapidly expanding, offered the exciting possibility of a single, internationally agreed system of weights and measures.

1.4 Development of the metric system

These advantages were quickly appreciated, and the metric system began to spread rapidly. It was first adopted in the Netherlands, then in Italy, then in Spain and Portugal, from where it spread to South America; by 1872 no less than thirty nations were represented at a meeting called to discuss improvements in the definitions of the primary units. It is now the official system in 103 sovereign states. A further 28 countries, most of which are in some way associated with the United Kingdom, have chosen to adopt the metric system. In this country the legal definitions of most of our own units are expressed in terms of the metric system; the earlier independent definitions were abandoned in 1963. (*see* Figure 1, page 8)

It is a striking fact that no country, once it has adopted the metric system, has ever reverted to its former system or changed to any other. Historians sometimes draw attention to a single curious exception: France itself had second thoughts right at the start, when the system was only a few years old; but the mood of indecision did not last very long.

Figure 1

The Metric World, 1971

Metric

Afghanistan
Albania
Algeria
Andorra
Arab Republic
  of Egypt
Argentina
Austria
Belgium
Bolivia
Brazil
Bulgaria
Burundi
Cambodia
Cameroon
Central African
  Republic
Chad
Chile
China (People's
  Republic)
Colombia
Congo (Republic)
Costa Rica
Cuba
Cyprus
Czechoslovakia
Dahomey
Denmark
Dominican
  Republic
East Germany
Ecuador
El Salvador
Equatorial
  Guinea
Ethiopia
Finland

Formosa
France
Gabon
Germany (Federal
  Republic)
Greece
Guatemala
Guinea
Haiti
Honduras
Hungary
Iceland
India
Indonesia
Iran
Iraq
Israel
Italy
Ivory Coast
Japan
Jordan
Korea
Kuwait
Laos
Lebanon
Libya
Liechtenstein
Luxembourg
Malagasy Republic
Mali
Malta GC
Mauritania
Mauritius
Mexico
Monaco
Mongolian People's
  Republic
Morocco

Nepal
Netherlands
Nicaragua
Niger
Norway
Panama
Paraguay
Peru
Philippines
Poland
Portugal
Romania
Rwanda
San Marino
Saudi Arabia
Senegal
Somalia
Spain
Sudan
Sweden
Switzerland
Syria
Thailand
Togo
Tunisia
Turkey
USSR
Upper Volta
Uruguay
Venezuela
Vietnam
Western Samoa
Yugoslavia
Zaire

Going Metric

Australia
Bahrain
Botswana
Canada
Fiji
Ghana
Guyana
Ireland (Republic)
Kenya
Lesotho

Malawi
Malaysia
Maldives (Republic)
New Zealand
Nigeria
Oman
Pakistan
Qatar
Singapore
South Africa

Sri Lanka
Swaziland
Tanzania
Trinidad & Tobago
Uganda
United Arab
  Emirates
United Kingdom
Zambia

This examination of the origin of the metric system has been largely against the background of conditions as they existed a hundred or more years ago. Since then education has spread to far larger numbers of people, and the complexity of our society has led to a staggering increase in the amount of arithmetic carried out in industry, commerce and our daily life. The same basic advantages of a decimal system still hold good. The preference for decimal arithmetic is reinforced by the increasing use of aids to calculation such as the slide-rule, logarithm tables and calculating machines, all of which use decimals. The abacus is still used to great advantage in some countries—again on a decimal basis. The recent adoption of a decimal currency in the United Kingdom is one more step in what can now be seen as the inexorable advance of decimal arithmetic.

The remarkable progress of science and technology in the last hundred years has made entirely new demands upon the language of units, and raised problems unforeseen by the originators of the metric system. The first metric units were intended mainly for use in simple commercial transactions. The discoveries of science introduced entirely new concepts, such as force, pressure, energy, heat, power, viscosity, electric current, for each of which a suitable unit had to be devised. At first the choice was based largely on the need for a simple, readily utilised definition; thus the metric unit of heat was defined as the amount required to raise the temperature of a gramme of water by one degree centigrade (now Celsius); it was called the calorie. The same requirements had of course to be met in non-metric systems, and in the imperial system the heat unit was similarly defined as the amount needed to raise the temperature of one pound of water by one degree Fahrenheit; it was called the British thermal unit. It may be remarked that decimal ideas had by then sufficiently established themselves to inhibit the development of series of units related by non-decimal numbers. Thus the only additional heat unit to achieve recognition in this country was the therm, which is equal to 100 000 British thermal units.

During this period of rapid development, scientists in non-metric countries abandoned the struggle to invent their own units for all the new quantities, and began to use the metric system. They failed to persuade non-scientists, including engineers, to follow their example. As a result, since that time two systems of units have existed side by side in non-metric countries, and all our children whose education has progressed beyond an elementary level have had to learn both the metric system and the imperial. This decision by the scientific community had another important effect, in that branches of industry based on the new scientific discoveries naturally made use of the scientific metric units, and saw no reason to develop imperial units. In particular, electrical engineering adopted the ampere, volt, ohm and watt, all of them metric units, and these have become familiar to the general public as well.

Even in the metric system the new units were added rather un-systematically, without appreciating that arbitrary, non-decimal numbers relating one unit with another were thereby being introduced. Different sections of technology introduced their own units independently. For the important quantities of work, heat, energy and power, a variety of units sprang up, and were extensively used. Electrical engineers used the kilowatt for power, whereas mechanical engineers used the horse-power; and since one horse-power (metric) equals 0.735 499 kilowatt it is clear that one of the cardinal principles of the metric system had been forgotten. Many other examples could be given, and the situation was no better in the imperial system.

1.5 Origin and development of the International System
In a sense, this difficulty had been foreseen as early as 1832, when the German physicist Gauss proposed a system of so-called 'absolute' units. He asserted that most of the new units which were being devised were unnecessary, since acceptable alternatives could be formed from already existing units. If, for example, the agreed unit for length is the metre, and the unit for time is the second, a unit for speed can be formed by dividing the one by the other, giving the metre per second. In the same way a possible unit for acceleration is the (metre per second) per second. Two new units have thus been added to the system without increasing the number of arbitrarily defined, independent units. This idea was obvious enough, and represented no more than the current practice. Gauss went further and suggested that a unit of force could be formed from the product of unit mass with unit acceleration, in accordance with one of Newton's 'laws of motion', and indeed that a whole system of units could be built up in this way from three independent units, namely, those of length, mass and time.

These ideas gradually found support in scientific circles and it was agreed that the three units forming the basis of the new system could be the centimetre, the gramme and the second. The system was further developed, with the new technology of electricity principally in mind, by a committee set up by the British Association for the Advancement of

Science, and the ensuing proposals were endorsed at an international meeting in 1881. They became known as the 'cgs' system; it has been widely used by scientists, many of whom have regarded the names 'metric system' and 'cgs system' as almost synonymous.

The cgs system did not please everybody. Many branches of technology went their own ways, using units such as the calorie and the horse-power even though alternative cgs units were available. Electrical engineers accepted it in part; they found that some of the cgs units were of an inconvenient size for industrial usage, so they settled on certain decimal multiples, in accordance with metric principles; instead, however, of using the prefix language they invented new names: thus the 'erg', the cgs unit for energy, was too small, so they agreed to use a unit ten million times larger, which they called the 'joule'.

This rather unsatisfactory situation eventually gave rise to a renewed interest in Gauss's original proposal, but this time it was suggested that a more convenient system could be based on the metre, kilogramme and second, rather than the centimetre, gramme and second. It became known as the 'MKS system', and was extensively adopted, principally by electrical engineers, and some of its features were found acceptable in other disciplines as well. By now the subject of unit-systems was becoming much more clearly understood, and further contributions (notably by the Italian Giorgi) led eventually to the development of a new and comprehensive system based on the MKS system. This was formally approved at a meeting of the international General Conference of Weights and Measures in 1960 and given the name International System of Units. The accepted abbreviation in all languages is 'SI'. (*see* Figure 2, page 12)

The arrival of SI on the scene restores, in effect, the purity and simplicity of the original metric concept, with the added advantage that it covers the whole range of science and technology and all other applications. Its salient characteristics are:

1 Like the earlier metric systems, it uses the principle of a single primary unit for each quantity together with the decimal prefixes, and is therefore suitable for decimal arithmetic.

2 Unlike the earlier metric systems, it is based on the smallest practicable number of independently defined units, all other units being formed by combining these independent units together; as a result, there is only one primary unit for each quantity, so that it is never necessary to convert from one unit to another.

11

Figure 2

Chronological Development
of the International System

10—5000 BC	Earliest indications of measurement
3—2000 BC	Clear evidence of units
1000 BC	Evidence of decimal counting
0	
	Decimal notation for whole numbers
1000 AD	
1500	
	Stevenius : decimals proposed for fractions
1600	
	Napier : decimal point
	Gunter : decimalised "chain"
	Mouton : decimal weights and measures proposed
1700	
	Decimal currency in USA
	Metric system founded in France
1800	
	Gauss : "absolute" system proposed
	Metric system enforced in France
	Metre Convention
	"cgs" system established
1900	"MKS" system established
	Many new units agreed
	"MKSA" or Giorgi system established
	International System established
	Imperial units defined in terms of SI units
2000	

3   In forming new units in this way, no numerical factors are introduced, so that the system is almost entirely free from numbers other than ten.

4   The system can be extended indefinitely, and provides an acceptable, unique unit-language for all countries, industries, trades, scientific disciplines, indeed for any conceivable activity which requires the use of units of measurement.

The superiority of the International System over the earlier metric systems, and still more over the imperial system, can be demonstrated most effectively by quoting examples of technical calculations of some complexity. Almost more important, however, is the fact that these advantages, together with the great simplification introduced by the principle of one unit only for each quantity, makes it possible for the original grand conception of a single unit system for all purposes throughout the world to be fulfilled. The advantages that would follow can scarcely be exaggerated. There are clear signs that this possibility has seized the imagination of scientists all over the world, and the impetus of the movement to replace the conventional metric system by the International System is growing rapidly. It has already had its effect on legislation in a number of countries, and several have now declared their intention to abandon non-SI units within a few years.

It has been made clear that the basis of the change to metric in this country is the change from imperial units to SI units. In the following discussion, therefore, wherever the distinction between SI and the earlier metric systems is significant, it is the former that will be considered.

1.6 The metric debate

Public discussion about metrication in this country which followed the Government's support of industry's decision to go metric has brought to light a good deal of misunderstanding and confusion about the metric system itself and about certain possible consequences of its adoption. Before going into too much detail, therefore, it will be useful to examine one or two issues of a general nature.

In the first place, it should be understood that the metric system and the imperial system are just two different ways of measuring things; that and nothing more. A man may be described as being 5 ft $9\frac{1}{2}$ in tall or 177 cm tall, but his actual height remains the same—neither system will add one cubit to his stature! Anything can be measured or made according to either system; the adoption of a particular system does not *necessarily* have any impact at all on what we do, any more than a football match is altered by the language in which the commentator is speaking. The point of substance here may be exemplified as follows: if British tables are at present 6 feet long it does not follow automatically that, after metrication, they will all be 2 metres long. Criticism of the metric system itself on the grounds that developments of this nature would *inevitably* follow is misplaced.

Nevertheless such developments might very well follow, for the obvious reason that when a quantity is to some degree arbitrary it is natural to give it a size which can be simply expressed in terms of the units used. It is easier to quote 2 metres as the length of a table rather than 1.83 metres, and there will be a tendency to use round numbers accordingly. Furthermore, standard sizes in metric countries are generally aligned with the metric system, so that the trend towards international standards will also urge us in this direction. The point is therefore by no means devoid of significance, but it is important to note that such changes are quite voluntary; they do not of necessity follow the adoption of a new system of measurement. The standard gauge of railway track throughout the world has for many years been 4 ft $8\frac{1}{2}$ inches or 1.435 metres; neither figure is in the least 'round', but there is not the slightest possibility that the gauge will be altered just for that reason.

This is a very important point, since much of the resistance to the metric system in this country and the USA was derived not so much from any disapproval of the system itself but from a fear of the change in standard sizes and so on which might result from its adoption.

The second issue concerns the belief that a struggle is now in progress between the imperial system and the metric system to see which will eventually emerge as the victor and be used throughout the world. It has been argued that the advantages of the metric system could be countered by improving the imperial system, and that the resulting system—with the weight of British and American support behind it—might in course of time be adopted by everyone. This naturally implies the possibility that the metric system might one day become obsolete.

There does not appear to be a shred of evidence to support this idea. In the first place, the metric system is used by scientists in all countries without exception. The International System has been developed and formally agreed by an international body which includes distinguished representatives from the UK and the USA. In our Weights and Measures Act of 1963 the principal imperial units—the yard and the pound—are defined in terms of metric units, in such a way as to take advantage of any subsequent improvements in definition [3]. The attempt to maintain independent imperial standards of comparable precision has long ago been abandoned. The idea that the world of science will one day forsake the metric system is sheer moonshine. Even in the USA—of all countries perhaps most deeply rooted in the inch-pound system—the principal scientific organisations have long supported the use of the metric system; reports from the National Bureau of Standards are expressed in metric units; and the National Aeronautics and Space Administration issued an instruction in 1964 that all formal reports of scientific work were to be presented in terms of the International System [4].

The possibility of improving the imperial system until it rivals the standard of the metric system is another mirage. To quote first from the Report of the Hodgson Committee, which examined the Weights and Measures problem on behalf of the Board of Trade in 1951: 'It is, however, hardly correct to talk of the "imperial system" in quite the same way as one talks of the "metric system". The latter forms one compact, closely-defined and universally-recognised system of measurement under the guidance of an international body consisting of representatives of all countries subscribing to its activities; whereas the imperial system is really a conglomeration of units which have in the past been found convenient for particular types of measurement and which have, over the years, been linked together to form a rough whole' [5].

Certainly some of the major defects of the imperial system could be removed with advantage. This process is in fact going on all the time: within the last few years the bushel, peck, pennyweight and scruple have ceased to be legally usable for purposes of trade. There are a number of serious differences between the units used in the USA and in this country, and these could be ironed out in the direction of simplicity; for example, the American ton of 2000 pounds might supersede ours of 2240 pounds, and we might adopt the streamlined hundredweight of 100 pounds (the cental). The idea of having a system of linear measure based on the foot and its decimals, or on the inch and a new foot equal to 10 inches, and abandoning all other length units, has been seriously suggested. It will be noticed that these are all steps in the direction of decimalisation—following the example of the metric system. The virtual impossibility of making a success of such ideas becomes apparent as soon as one begins to explore the intricacies of the International System, with its closely interlocking units for all branches of technology. To take one example only, in the International System the base units kilogramme, metre and second are combined to form a unit for mechanical power, and the result is the watt—already well established as an electrical unit. To develop a comparable system based, say, on the foot, pound and hour, and to persuade the world to accept it, would be an almost superhuman task at this stage. Quoting again from the Hodgson Report: 'It has been suggested to us that a possible compromise would be to decimalise the imperial system, so as to obtain one of the major benefits of the metric system whilst retaining the historically valuable associations of the imperial yard and pound and enabling much of the existing weighing and measuring equipment to be kept in use. We consider, however, that the confusion and inconvenience of such a step would be only a little less than that which would be caused by a complete change to the metric system, without conferring in return the advantages of world-wide uniformity. Certain improvements can and should be made in the imperial system if it is to continue to exist; but we are convinced that if a major change is to be made, it can only be towards the full adoption of the metric system.'

The argument that the magnitude of the American industrial effort might prove a decisive factor can also be dismissed; all the evidence in the last hundred years points the other way. In 1920, during one of the many revivals of the metrication debate in the USA, it was remarked that 55% of the world's production of machine tools was in terms of the inch, clear evidence, it was argued, that nothing could stop the advance of the inch; but in fact in 1965 it was found that the proportion had declined to 26% [6]. In 1968 Congress instituted a study of the advantages and disadvantages of the increased use of the metric system to the United States. The report of this study was published in July 1971. It recommended to Congress that the United States should change to the metric system through a co-ordinated national programme and that Congress should establish a date ten years ahead by which time the USA would be predominantly metric [7].

As another indication, in the nineteen-thirties the growth of industry in Japan led to the decision to replace the traditional units by the metric system, but there was much opposition and inertia to be overcome and when the war started the process of conversion was far from complete. After the war the disorganised country was occupied by Americans, bringing with them the inch-pound system, which became firmly established. In due course, however, the Japanese, having experienced both systems, renewed their decision to adopt the metric system, and it was soon afterwards made compulsory.

The alternatives the world faces are, therefore, not 'metric system or another' but 'metric system or metric system *plus* another', since the metric countries will never adopt the inch-pound units, and the non-metric countries cannot ignore the metric system. This has a most important bearing on educational matters. The metric system is already used in this country for all scientific work and for pharmacy, and is becoming increasingly used for other applications. With every year that passes more and more of our young people going on to higher education have to be familiar with the metric system. The growth of international trade means that more people have to retain a familiarity with it after their formal education has ended. If the imperial system of units is retained in this country a continually increasing proportion of the population will have to learn to use *both* systems.

One last general point may usefully be made at this stage. It is difficult for us to form a dispassionate, objective judgement on the relative merits of the metric and imperial systems, because we are so much more familiar with the one than the other. Pounds and ounces, feet and inches seem second nature to us and we have long ago forgotten the difficulty we experienced in mastering them. For this reason, in various parts of this study certain elementary arithmetical procedures will be explained in much greater detail than might appear necessary, in order to draw attention to the considerable amount of mental effort that habit makes us take for granted. The use of the metric system requires us to develop a different set of techniques and skills, and it may be accepted that an immediate switch to the metric system for all purposes would create acute problems, but we should be very careful not to allow this to distort our judgement concerning the long-term effects of such a change. The Hodgson Report [5] makes the point in this way: 'the element of human inertia is often ignored; and the contention that a separate system is suitable for particular purposes may often be based on an assessment in which the real long-term advantages of a change to complete uniformity are obscured by the probable immediate inconveniences of the disturbance'.

2
Advantages in Everyday Use

The subject of measurement units means different things to different people. In discussing the development of the International System, for instance, considerations were introduced which might well seem a matter of complete indifference to all but a handful of scientists. In order to avoid confusion the metric and imperial systems will be compared, in separate sections of this study, at three different levels of complexity. In the present section their use will be considered at the most elementary and universal level; the heading 'Everyday use' will be interpreted as implying 'everyman use' as well, and with very few exceptions this restricts the field to the domestic scene.

2.1 Criteria for comparison

It will be convenient to start by considering the broad principles underlying the use of units at this level, and the criteria which may be invoked in comparing different systems. The primary function, as always, is that of introducing precision into the handling of quantities. The housewife who buys a pint of milk is not prepared to accept an indefinite amount; she expects a quantity lying between very narrow limits, because only then can she rely on past experience to tell her how long it will last her family, and what impact its purchase will have upon her budget. This insistence on precision is of such importance that 'weights and measures' has for centuries figured in our legislation; an inspectorate exists, with representatives in every town, to supervise these matters; and significant errors by the vendor, even when inadvertent, are severely punished.

Precision, however, does not in itself furnish a very useful criterion for comparison, since (at this level at any rate) both the metric and imperial systems are more than adequately defined, both scientifically and legally.

Possible criteria begin to emerge when one considers the *size* and *number* of the units available. As an example, it would be awkward, to say the least, if the mile were the only available unit of length. This is chiefly because units are so intimately connected with communication. We are constantly having to use them in speech and writing. There is nothing wrong in saying that a man's height is 1/2640 mile or 0.000 379 mile; it is just very inconvenient. For the same reason the *names* of the units are important. In both speech and writing they should be simple, brief and free from any possibility of confusion. Acceptable abbreviations should be available, and one is also entitled to consider the length and appearance of a quantity statement of reasonable precision.

The ability to state a quantity is of course only the beginning; behind every statement lies a measurement. Two distinct kinds of measurement may be identified. The first is the measurement of a 'given' quantity, as when the butcher weighs a joint of meat in order to calculate its price. The second is the measurement of a 'required' quantity, as when the grocer weighs out a pound of rice. The two often go together, for a man may first measure the width of a cupboard (the given quantity) as 2 ft $9\frac{1}{2}$ in, and then mark off a shelf of this length (the required quantity) from a longer plank. In each case the essential basic operation is the same: the location of a position on a scale, so constructed that to every position there corresponds a unique number related to the system of units being used. The nature of the *scale* depends on the units used, and its convenience, legibility and so on furnish another criterion for comparison.

At the domestic level, measurement and statement are often the end of the matter, but occasionally a calculation follows; by far the commonest is the determination of a price from the product of a weight and a cost per unit weight. Convenience in *calculation* is therefore another possible criterion.

As a final point one might consider the extent to which a system contains *alternative units* not differing greatly in size. This tends to hamper communication in various ways. Both this and the preceding criterion are closely associated with the numerical relations between units, a consideration which is fundamental to the whole question of unit systems.

The number of different kinds of quantity that are measured in everyday usage is very small. The most important are weight, capacity and volume, which are associated with the purchase of food and fuel, closely followed by length and area; temperature is also encountered, though precision is seldom very important; time is of course universal but is in a rather special category. These are few enough to admit of individual consideration, and their importance justifies such treatment.

2.2 Weight

In the imperial system the commonest units for weight are the pound and the ounce. The stone is used to a limited extent, principally for personal weighing and occasionally for the purchase of commodities such as potatoes; the hundredweight and ton are used chiefly for solid fuels. These units cover a range of 35 840 : 1 in steps of 16, 14, 8 and 20. They typify the imperial system, in that a generous variety of units is provided but the numbers relating them are all different (and do not include 10). There are indeed many other weight units available; the Weights and Measures Act 1963 [3], which lists the units of length, area, volume, capacity and mass or weight which are lawful for use for trade in the UK, refers to those just mentioned, and adds the cental, quarter, dram, grain and ounce (troy), making a total of 10. These additional units are not normally used outside restricted circles and are almost unknown to most people.

The Act recognises six metric units (apart from the metric carat which is used only for jewellery), namely the milligramme, gramme, hectogramme, kilogramme, quintal and tonne. Only three of these appear to be necessary for domestic use, namely the gramme, which is about $\frac{1}{25}$ ounce, the kilogramme, which is a little more than 2 pounds, and the tonne, which is slightly less than the imperial ton. The ratios between them are 1000 in each case, giving an overall range of 1 million. The following are examples of comparative statements in both systems, to give a better idea of magnitudes (these are not intended to be exact equivalents):

1 oz of cooking fat	25 g
$\frac{1}{4}$ lb of tea	125 g
$\frac{1}{2}$ lb of butter	250 g
1 lb of flour	500 g
2 lb of sugar	1 kg
1 stone of potatoes	6 kg
1 cwt of cement	50 kg
$\frac{1}{2}$ ton of coal	$\frac{1}{2}$ tonne.

It will be apparent that no difficulty arises in finding a convenient metric unit for any of these quantities; the numbers are sometimes larger, because of the bigger interval between successive units, but they never exceed three figures and continental experience shows that no trouble is experienced on this account. On the other hand the number of units has been reduced from five to three, and the effort required to memorise them is trivial compared with the effort of learning and handling five units and the associated conversion factors 16, 14, 8, 20, 112 and 2240. Further, the smallness of the ratios between the imperial units results in the frequent use of alternatives, such as ounces or pounds, pounds or stones, stones or hundredweights, and conversion—particularly when it involves 16 or 14—is a nuisance. (*see* Figure 3, page 22)

The names of the imperial units are of course straightforward enough and may well appear preferable to the metric names, but we must be careful not to be misled by familiarity. In everyday speech in metric countries the three common units are usually called gramme, kilo and tonne; one could hardly imagine simpler names (and there are only three of them). The correct, scientific name for the tonne is the megagramme, and this emphasises the logical way in which the names of the metric system are chosen; a single unit for each quantity (the gramme in this instance) together with a single set of names for the prefixes (which are used for all quantities).

In writing, the names of units are usually given in abbreviated form. The abbreviations for the imperial units are oz, lb, st, cwt, and ton, and it is intriguing to note that one of these is not an abbreviation at all, and that three bear no resemblance to the full names. As usual, they just have to be learnt by rote. The metric abbreviations are g, kg, and t or Mg; g for gramme is obvious, as is t for tonne, and the prefix abbreviations k and M have only to be learnt once since they are used with all metric units.

The contrast between the two systems becomes more striking when we consider statements of greater precision. Take 3 lb $5\frac{1}{2}$ oz for example; this becomes 1.52 kg—seven typing spaces instead of 10; 12 stone 3 lb 3 oz becomes 77.6 kg. Many still more impressive examples could be quoted, and we can still find dinosaurs such as 2 ton 13 cwt 3 qr 1 st 6 lb 3 oz in arithmetic books!

2.3 Volume and capacity
In the Weights and Measures Act, volume and capacity are treated

Figure 3

Comparison of Imperial and Metric Units for Length, Weight and Volume

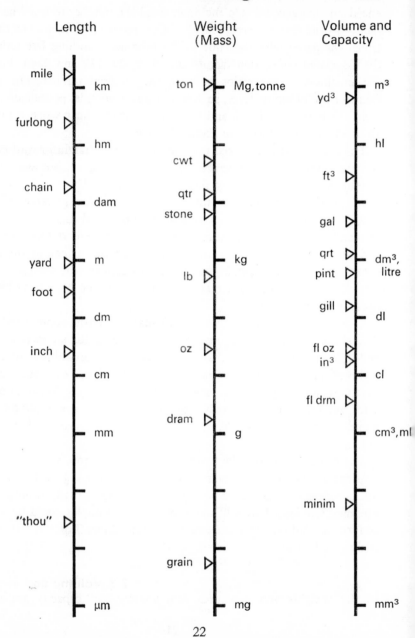

separately, though to the scientist they are indistinguishable. Measurement by capacity is a very ancient practice. The simplest way of measuring a quantity of wheat or apples is to see how many standard containers can be filled. The 'capacity' of the container is accordingly a unit, and this practice gave rise to our system of 'dry measure'. The same procedure can be followed for measuring liquids, and another set of units was produced which became known as 'liquid measure'. It was not until later that the practice developed of determining the amount of space in containers by multiplying three length dimensions together; this resulted in a set of units of volume. In fact only one physical quantity is involved, and the relation between a unit of capacity and a unit of volume is a pure number.

The Act lists the following imperial units: for capacity, the gallon, quart, pint, gill and fluid ounce; and for volume, the cubic inch, cubic foot and cubic yard. Everyday usage is limited to the pint and the gallon, with the quart and the gill—and possibly the fluid ounce—less frequently used; the three volume units may be encountered occasionally. The ratios involved for capacity are fluid ounce $\times 5 =$ gill, $\times 4 =$ pint, $\times 2 =$ quart, $\times 4 =$ gallon, giving a range of only 160 for five distinct units. The volume units introduce very awkward numbers: cubic inch $\times 1728 =$ cubic foot, $\times 27 =$ cubic yard. The complete independence of the two sets of units is revealed by the fact that 1 gallon equals 277.42 cubic inches (*see* Figure 3, page 22).

The metric units listed in the Act are the cubic centimetre, cubic decimetre, and cubic metre for volume, and the hectolitre, litre, decilitre, centilitre and millilitre for capacity. The distinction between volume and capacity is still there, a reflection perhaps of the fact that the metric system is now nearly 200 years old. There is an essential difference in that the litre is just another name for cubic decimetre (although the Weights and Measures Act does not yet recognise this). Bearing this in mind, the available units and their ratios are the millilitre $=$ cubic centimetre, $\times 10 =$ centilitre, $\times 10 =$ decilitre, $\times 10 =$ litre $=$ cubic decimetre, $\times 100 =$ hectolitre, $\times 10 =$ cubic metre. For everyday usage the litre and millilitre will probably be sufficient, though the decilitre is often used in metric countries. A litre is about $1\frac{3}{4}$ pints. The following is a comparable set of simple quantity statements (again not exact equivalents):

2 fluid ounces of olive oil	60 millilitres
1 gill of cream	150 millilitres
$\frac{1}{2}$ pint of milk	300 millilitres

1 quart of paint	1 litre
2 gallons of paraffin	10 litres
10 gallons of petrol	50 litres
100 gallons of fuel oil	500 litres.

In writing, some of the imperial units have abbreviations provided in regulations made under the Weights and Measures Act 1963. These are fl oz, pt, qt, gal. The metric abbreviations are simply ml and l. The volume abbreviations can employ cu for cubic or a raised 3, eg cu ft or ft³, cu m or m³. An expression such as 1 gal 3 pt 1 gill becomes compressed to 1860 ml or 1.86 l. This could equally well be expressed as 1860 cm³.

2.4 Length

The legal imperial units of length comprise the mile, furlong, chain, yard, foot and inch. Of these the furlong and chain are not in everyday use and we are normally content with the inch × 12 = foot, × 3 = yard, × 1760 = mile. The popular metric units are the millimetre × 10 = centimetre, × 100 = metre, × 1000 = kilometre; the decimetre is also included in the Weights and Measures Act, but is not often used (*see* Figure 3, page 22). Approximately corresponding quantity statements might be:

Thickness of plywood	$\frac{3}{16}$ inch	5 millimetres
Length of a nail	$1\frac{1}{2}$ inch	40 millimetres
Height of a table	2 feet 4 inches	70 centimetres
Height of a man	6 feet	180 centimetres
Width of a room	12 feet	4 metres
Length of a garden	30 yards	30 metres
Length of a road	2 miles	3 kilometres
Distance between towns	150 miles	240 kilometres

The imperial names inch, foot, etc, are simple enough, but as usual quite unrelated, and have to be memorised individually. The metric names involve only the metre, together with the usual prefixes. In abbreviated form we have in, ft, yd, mile, to which little exception can be taken except for their variety; the metric abbreviations are mm, cm, m, km, which could scarcely be simpler.

The operation of measuring a length provides a useful illustration of another contrast between the two systems. Suppose a man wants to measure the size of a room. He will very likely use a yard measure, but will count in feet as he proceeds across the floor: 3, 6, 9, 12 ft, plus 2 ft 3 in = 14 ft 3 in long; width, 3, 6, 9, plus 1 ft 6 in = 10 ft 6 in wide. If he is using the metric system he would have a metre measure and he might count in centimetres or metres—it is immaterial because the numbers are the same: 100, 200, 300, 400, plus 40, giving 440 cm in all (or 1, 2, 3, 4 m plus 40 cm giving 4.40 m), and then 1, 2, 3 m plus 60 cm giving 3.60 m. Note that he is simply counting 1, 2, 3 in the ordinary way and has no need to multiply by 3 at any stage. His final expression can be written in a variety of ways, but is always shorter and neater. It is also capable of extension very simply to a greater degree of precision if this should be necessary; by adding a further figure 3.60 m becomes 3.603 m for example, thereby achieving a precision of 1 millimetre, which is $\frac{1}{25}$ inch. In the imperial system, for anything which requires a better precision than the inch we normally use fractions. We shall look at this again a little later on.

It is sometimes argued that the absence from the metric system of a unit of similar length to the foot is a serious defect, but this does not really stand up to examination; the metre is only three times as big, which is surely near enough. This is merely a reaction based on unfamiliarity.

2.5 Area

The units of area listed in the Act are the square mile, acre, rood, square yard, square foot and square inch, all quite familiar apart from the rood, which is seldom used outside agriculture. Leaving this aside, the ratios are square inch $\times$ 144 = square foot, $\times$ 9 = square yard, $\times$ 4840 = acre, $\times$ 640 = square mile; the man-in-the-street will probably not remember 4840 or 640, since he rarely uses them. The metric units listed are the square millimetre, square centimetre, square decimetre, square metre, are, dekare and hectare, of which the square centimetre (about 0.15 square inch), the square metre (about 1.2 square yard) and the hectare ($2\frac{1}{2}$ acres) are likely to be most frequently used; the ratios between them are square centimetre $\times$ 10 000 = square metre, $\times$ 10 000 = hectare. Roughly corresponding statements might be:

area of a room	130 square feet	12 square metres
plan area of a house	1200 square feet	110 square metres
area of a garden	350 square yards	300 square metres
area of a field	15 acres	6 hectares

The names of these units are mostly made up of the names of length

25

units plus the word square except that, oddly enough, both systems introduce an entirely new name for the agrarian unit. The hectare, however, is a regular member of its series; it is equal to 10 000 square metres, ie a square of a side 100 metres, whereas the acre at 4840 square yards is out on its own. In abbreviated form, in each series one may write sq before the corresponding length abbreviation (sq ft, sq yd), but the preferred form in the metric system uses instead a raised 2, giving cm², m². The hectare is written ha.

2.6 Temperature

The Weights and Measures Act does not refer to temperature because it does not normally arise in commercial transactions. The imperial system is associated with the Fahrenheit scale, and the metric system with the Celsius scale (the latter is exactly the same as the former centigrade scale, the name having been changed to avoid confusion with a system used in some countries, of dividing plane angles so that 100 grades = 1 right angle). There is really little to choose between the two scales; the Celsius degree is nearly twice as big as the Fahrenheit degree, and it is sometimes said that this is a disadvantage since, on the Fahrenheit scale, greater precision can be achieved when quoting temperatures in whole numbers. The argument cannot be taken very seriously as we seldom need greater precision than that afforded by the Celsius scale and where it is essential, for example in taking the temperature of a patient, the degree is decimalised (in both systems) and the Celsius scale is then quite adequate. It has in fact now been adopted as standard practice in our hospitals. It could be argued that the choice in the Celsius scale of 0 °C and 100 °C respectively for the freezing and boiling points of water may be helpful at domestic level, since these particular temperatures are so important. In considering the temperature of a deep-freeze cabinet, where the temperature must be below freezing point, a starting point of 0 °C may be thought more sensible than the Fahrenheit figure of 32 °F.

2.7 Time

The measurement of time introduces a number of unusual features. There are two quite distinct types of measurement; first 'the time', ie a position on the continuous scale, as for example 1066, December 25, half-past three; and secondly a time interval, eg four minutes to boil an egg, an hour and a half to wait for the train, a fortnight's holiday. Further, our lives are governed by two astronomical phenomena outside our control, namely, the motion of the earth about its axis and round the sun, so that the day and the year are units which we could not avoid even if we wished to. The subdivision of the year into months and weeks, and the day into hours, minutes and seconds are arbitrary, and a perfect system might make more use of decimal divisions; such a system was indeed proposed when the metric system was first devised but the upheaval resulting from any alteration now would be inconceivable and the advantages would be limited. These matters are not really the concern of the metric system and there is no proposal to change our way of measuring time. The International System does have something to say about time units, as we shall see later, but this only applies to technical matters.

2.8 Scales of measurement

An important aspect of unit systems, which has already been briefly referred to but not fully discussed, is that of the scales used when making measurements. These appear in almost every type of measurement; for length we have the foot-rule, yardstick and so on; for weight we have the balance-scale with a pointer moving across it; for volume and capacity, the graduated vessel with a liquid level as indicator; for time, the clock-face with the hour, minute and second hands; for temperature, a scale with the mercury level as indicator. An accurate scale will be divided into as many intervals as possible consistent with comfortable reading.

In constructing such a scale in the metric system, tens are invariably used as a basis for this subdivision. This is in line with our normal process of counting, and is the method we naturally use when given a free hand. For example, in both the Fahrenheit and Celsius temperature scales, where the intervals correspond to degrees, we arrange them in tens and assign numbers accordingly—50, 60, 70 (*see* Figure 4, Scale A), etc. The imperial system forces us away from this simple procedure. A typical folding rule, for example, is a yard long; it is labelled 3 feet, but is divided into inches, which are numbered successively from 1 to 36; if we read off 27 inches we shall probably find ourselves saying 2 feet 3 inches. Each inch is divided into 2, 4 and 8 parts, by graduations of three different lengths (Figure 4, Scale B). A typical household balance has a scale divided first into pounds, then each pound is divided into 16 ounces by graduations of two different lengths (Figure 4, Scale C). A balance for personal weighing has a scale divided first into stones, each of which is divided into 14 pounds (Figure 4, Scale D). A pint measuring-jug is graduated first into 4 quarter-pints each of which is subdivided into

Figure 4

Variety of Imperial Scales Compared With Metric

A

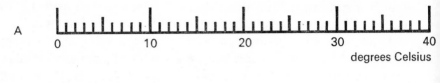

0   10   20   30   40

degrees Celsius

B

0   1   2   3   4

inches and eighths

C

0    $\frac{1}{4}$ $\frac{1}{2}$ $\frac{3}{4}$ 1 $\frac{1}{4}$ $\frac{1}{2}$ $\frac{3}{4}$ 2

pounds and ounces

D

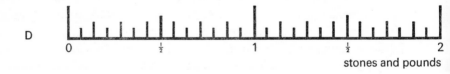

0       $\frac{1}{2}$ 1 $\frac{1}{2}$ 2

stones and pounds

E

0   5 $\frac{1}{2}$ 15   1   5 $\frac{1}{2}$ 15   2

pints and fluid ounces

F

0   1   2   3   4

kilogrammes

G

0   100   200   300   400

millilitres

5 fluid ounces (Figure 4, Scale E). These scales are all different, and we cannot develop quite the same degree of facility in reading them that we might if they were identical. (The pound/stone scale is particularly awkward, and has long been abandoned in America.) All metric scales on the other hand are essentially the same; they are all divided decimally, each unit being subdivided into tenths, generally with only the mid-position ($\frac{5}{10} = \frac{1}{2}$) accentuated. Scales A, F and G in Figure 4 are identical, though the numbers and units are quite different. Apart from this helpful uniformity, there are reasons for believing that the decimal scale is easier to read than any of the others. This point will be examined in greater detail later.

2.9 Units in the home

In many ways the domestic scene may be said to approximate to the simple measurement conditions which gave rise to the imperial system. It would be rather surprising if in this area our familiar units were totally inadequate, or the metric system overwhelmingly superior. The principal domestic activities which make use of units are the purchase of household goods such as food and fuel; cooking, dressmaking and soft furnishing generally; and do-it-yourself matters such as decorating and woodwork. The housewife will buy a pound of butter and subsequently weigh out six ounces for a cake; she will buy a quart of milk and measure a pint-and-a-half for a custard. On occasion she might measure the approximate height of a window in feet, and buy a sufficient length of material in yards to make curtains; when making them up she will measure more accurately, in feet and inches. Her husband will measure the size of a room in feet and work out how much emulsion paint he needs for the walls, on the basis of so many gallons to the square yard; he may dilute the paint by adding a pint of water to the gallon.

To a considerable extent nowadays units are in effect by-passed, since commodities are increasingly prepacked in quantities which may or may not be simply related to familiar units. The purchaser will either estimate by eye the adequacy of the quantity offered, or rely on past experience on the assumption that the contents are always the same. We are content to buy a 'bottle' of whisky knowing that we shall get a standard quantity, and we rarely bother to note that it is '$26\frac{2}{3}$ fluid ounces' (few of us in fact know what a fluid ounce is).

Everyday life thus makes very little demand on units other than that they shall be familiar and of a convenient size. Nevertheless even at this relatively simple level the metric system has certain advantages to offer, each one small in itself but adding up to a significant total. Some have already been touched upon. There are fewer metric units to learn and remember; their names and abbreviations are a little simpler, a little more logical; the scales are uniform and rather easier to read. The major difference between the two systems, the much more complicated relations between the imperial units, does not exert anything like its full force at this level, but is not altogether without effect. We have already seen how, in measuring lengths, we leap with a skill born of long practice from inches to feet, feet to yards and back again; each step a tiny addition to the total effort and another opportunity for error (how often does someone confuse 1 ft 5 in with 15 in?). What will a 98 inch sheet look like on a 6 ft 3 in bed?—mental arithmetic is needed before we can tell. A newspaper reports public indignation over a proposal to convert 400 sq yards of a 24 acre playing field into a subway entrance: is this a significant proportion or not? The figures, as they stand, tell us very little.

Consider the customer in a supermarket who wishes to know which of three packets of detergent contains the largest quantity: one is labelled $1\frac{3}{4}$ lb, the second 1 lb 14 oz, and the third 29 oz. A tiresome little exercise in mental arithmetic is needed to effect a comparison, though all three statements are perfectly legitimate. The simpler relations between metric units prevent this kind of thing. Expressions such as 1.5 kg, 1400 g and 1 kg 450 g are instantly comparable, and even if, perversely, someone decides to use fractions, it is only necessary to remember the decimal equivalents $\frac{1}{2} = 0.5$, $\frac{1}{4} = 0.25$, and $\frac{3}{4} = 0.75$, since they are the same for all metric units. Contrast the imperial system, where $\frac{1}{2}$ lb = 8 oz, $\frac{1}{2}$ cwt = 56 lb, $\frac{1}{2}$ yard = 18 in, $\frac{1}{2}$ gallon = 4 pints, and so on; the variety is almost inexhaustible.

Some legally permissible units are virtually unknown to the general public. We have just mentioned the fluid ounce. The dram is another; nevertheless one may be offered a packet of potato crisps labelled '15 drams'. The metric system includes no such conundrums. In general the names are self-explanatory.

The householder buys solid fuel by the hundredweight or ton—the metric equivalent is the tonne; liquid fuel is sold by the gallon, which is comparable with the litre; these have already been sufficiently discussed. He buys electricity by the 'unit', which is in fact a kilowatt hour. The kilowatt is probably familiar enough to him as the rating of a single fire-bar. He is also aware that his main electricity supply comes at about 240 volts, and he knows all about 13 ampere plugs and 3 ampere fuses. These units—kilowatts, volts and amperes—are probably considered by some to be imperial, but in fact they are metric. No one ever bothered to develop imperial units for electricity and the metric units have been used in this country as in the rest of the world. So there is no change here.

Gas, on the other hand, is measured in the gas-meter by volume, and is accordingly sold by the cubic foot, but the Gas Board has to state the calorific value of the gas—the amount of heat available per cubic foot. This introduces our unit of heat, the British thermal unit or Btu, or more usually in this connection the therm, which equals 100 000 Btu. The metric unit is the joule, or more generally the megajoule (1 megajoule = 1 000 000 joules). Since 3.6 megajoules = 1 kilowatt hour there is a simple relation between these two units.

The average householder today is also a motorist, and this activity gives him a limited acquaintance with one or two units beyond those so far considered. He may know the size of his engine in litres or cubic centimetres; here he is already metric. A fully metric motorist buys his petrol by the litre ($= \frac{1}{5}$ gallon) and his oil by the half-litre ($= \frac{7}{8}$ pint). He measures distance travelled in kilometres ($= \frac{5}{8}$ mile) so that fuel consumption is quoted in km/litre and speed expressed in km/h. His tyre and oil pressures will probably be stated in terms of the bar, a unit familiar from its appearance on meteorological charts, where barometric pressures are quoted in millibars. A tyre pressure of 22 pounds per square inch appears as 1.5 bars. He may find the viscosity of his engine oil quoted in a metric unit. The metric motorist can, however, scarcely claim to be using these units of pressure and viscosity in any real, technical sense; they are little more than names to him, and the way in which they take their place in the International System does not concern him. The metric system therefore has no great advantage to offer at this level, and one must be content to observe that it provides units in every way as convenient as those of the imperial system while avoiding unnecessary and confusing variety.

2.10 Some criticisms of the metric system

It is sometimes claimed that the imperial system lends itself more readily to the use of fractions, which are said to be preferred by ordinary people of limited arithmetical ability. There is more than a suspicion here that we are making a virtue out of a necessity. To quote a length as 'two yards one foot six inches' is much more cumbersome, and takes longer to comprehend, than to say 'two and a half yards'; we find it helpful to work with a single unit if at all possible. In contrast, 2.5 m or 250 cm are just as intelligible as $2\frac{1}{2}$ m. Furthermore, whereas 2.3 m or even 2.35 m are equally concise and informative, there is really nothing one can do about 2 yd 1 ft 7 in, except perhaps to reduce it all to inches and then the number is too large and unwieldy. With imperial units, in fact, we may be said to take refuge in fractions whenever we can, because of the essential complexity of the system. Consider trying to work out the cost of three ounces of spice at £1·40 a pound: a very awkward little sum, so no wonder people prefer to think in terms of four ounces, ie $\frac{1}{4}$ lb. There is no difficulty at all in dealing with 80 g at £3·10 a kilogramme; multiply by 8 and shift the decimal point: 24·80 becomes £0·248, say 25p.

It is, of course, quite easy to use fractions with metric units if desired. The continental housewife buys her half-litre or quarter-kilo, and she can divide the price by 2 or 4. But those trained and brought up to use decimals usually prefer them to fractions.

Another red herring is concerned with the use of the dozen and with 'duo-decimal' arithmetic in general. The metric system is based on tens, and the only factors of ten are two and five. Twelve, on the other hand, has two, three, four and six as factors, and can therefore be subdivided in more generally useful ways. A case might, indeed, be made out for an entirely new system of counting based on twelves. The imperial system, however, is *not* based consistently upon twelve, which only appears in the inch-foot relation; it would therefore be necessary to change the imperial system almost entirely if a duo-decimal system were to be adopted. It is inconceivable to consider undertaking such a radical revolution which would leave this country even more out of step with the rest of the world.

It is common practice to pack articles in dozens or gross. Some people are under the impression that this practice is in some way prevented or discouraged when metric units are being used. This is entirely without foundation. The only point of any substance is the ease with which cost or weight calculations can be carried out when articles are reckoned in tens. The cost of ten books at £1·35 each is £13·50 at a glance. There is, however, no great difficulty in evaluating £1·35 × 12 = £16·20, so that if there is some other advantage in using the dozen or the gross, as in some packages, there is no reason at all why not.

A further objection to the metric system, often raised by those introduced to it for the first time, is that quantities which can be simply stated in imperial units become absurdly complicated in metric units. Many packaged goods now display the weight of their contents both in imperial and metric units, and it often seems that the imperial statement is much simpler than the metric: one pound as against 454 grammes, for instance, or 10 ounces and 283.5 grammes, or even 6 ounces and 170.11 grammes! With wearisome regularity attention is drawn to the 'absurdity of expecting the working man to call at the "local" for 0.568 261 litres of beer' instead of his customary pint. (Lloyd George apparently started this one!) [8] This sort of thing is, of course, in no sense a valid criticism of the metric system, but merely reflects the fact that the two systems are completely distinct and not related by simple numbers. Quantities are made up in this country in round numbers of imperial units, and the corresponding numbers in metric terms are inevitably non-round. In metric countries the position is reversed and quantities are made up in round numbers of metric units—1 kg, 200 g, $\frac{1}{2}$ litre—and would appear very odd in imperial units: 2.2046 lb, 7.0548 oz, 0.8799 pint. It may also be worth pointing out that these metric equivalents which are now appearing on packages are often unthinkingly expressed to a wholly unrealistic degree of precision. Consider for example, the '170.11 g' just mentioned, which argues a degree of precision of better than 1 in ten thousand. It is true that 1 lb = 0.453 592 37 kg, the exact, legal definition, but for very many purposes it would be quite good enough to put 1 lb = 0.45 kg: remember that 0.01 kg is only about $\frac{1}{3}$ ounce.

2.11 Calculations in the home
The domestic scene rarely produces a substantial calculation, partly no doubt because we shrink from the complications which arise when we attempt anything but the very simplest. We are, of course, faced almost every day with the task of estimating the cost of a required quantity from the price of a unit quantity; when the required quantity is a small round number, as it usually is, the resulting calculation is trivial, eg 3 pints of milk at 5p a pint. Minor difficulties often used to arise with our £sd currency, as for example finding the cost of 5 yards of material at £1.12.7. a yard, but these have now been left behind and such calculations are based on ordinary decimal arithmetic: 5 yards at £1·63 = £8·15. There remains only the comparatively unusual situation where the required quantity is not expressed in simple terms. Why, for example, do we submit to the extravagance of buying $3\frac{1}{2}$ yards of an expensive material when we really need only 3 yards 10 inches? Is it as much as anything because

of the bother of multiplying the price per yard by such an awkward figure ? In metric terms we might have 3.24 m at say £3·10 per metre, a simple decimal multiplication which anyone can do on a scrap of paper. With imperial units we should have to proceed somewhat as follows: 3 yards 10 inches $= 3\frac{10}{36}$ yards $= \frac{118}{36}$ yards, so that at £3·10 per yard the calculation becomes $\frac{118 \times 3·10}{36}$, a much more unpleasant affair.

The only other calculation which is at all likely in the domestic sphere is that of an area; for instance the area of a room, to find the cost of a floor-covering, or of a wall to estimate the quantity of paint required. We may compare 14 ft 4 in $\times$ 10 ft 10 in with 4.40 m $\times$ 3.60 m. The latter is just a matter of simple decimal arithmetic, but the former is a nuisance, and most householders will be content with an approximation such as 14 ft $\times$ 11 ft. Another way of regarding the superiority of the metric system is to note that it avoids the need for such rough-and-ready methods.

2.12 Units at school

At home we may evade the awkward calculation by a rough approximation. Our sons and daughters at school are not let off so lightly. We spend an average of about 15% of our lives as pupils. Despite the continual evolution of our educational system, the traditional 'three Rs' are still pre-eminent, for nobody can play a full part in our society without a reasonable proficiency in reading, writing and arithmetic. Nevertheless, these are but basic tools; there is much else of greater interest to learn, and the less time we take to acquire the elementary skills the better. A great deal of the time spent on arithmetic in school is devoted to learning about our system of weights and measures, and how it is used.

In 1860 an enquiry was sent to a considerable number of schoolmasters in England asking them to indicate, on a form, the amount of time actually spent by a typical pupil in various branches of arithmetic, and their estimate of the corresponding time if the metric system and a decimal currency were adopted [9]. The answers naturally varied widely, but it appeared on an average that 2 years and 10 months was spent on arithmetic, and that this could be cut to no more than nine or ten months. Anxious not to exaggerate, the supporters of the metric system claimed a saving of at least a year, and this has been repeated many times since. Somewhat more modest estimates have been made in recent years. An article in an American journal in 1960 asserts that 'teachers of arithmetic will agree that fully 25% of the child's time, and the teacher's as well, could be saved in arithmetic courses if the simple, interrelated metric decimal units were substituted for the English. Such monstrosities as proper fractions, numerators, least common denominators, greatest common divisors, and mixed numbers could be laid to rest with the celluloid collar and the ox-cart' [10].

In less flamboyant language, a Royal Society pamphlet of 1969 puts another aspect of the matter: 'The saving of time formerly spent in mastering the arithmetic of sterling and imperial weights and measures should make it possible to give children of this age a more balanced education, and in particular to introduce them to some livelier and more broadly-based aspects of mathematics' [11].

Perhaps the most reliable estimate of the time which would be saved by the adoption of the metric system comes from the British Association enquiry in 1960 [12]. A questionnaire was sent to a large number of school teachers. The conclusion reached from the replies was that, for children between 7 and 11, about 10% to 20% of the time spent on arithmetic would be saved, or about 5% of the *total* teaching time. The following extract is worth quoting: 'a quicker grasp of quantity if counting and measuring are done in the same system. This would make arithmetic more logical, unified, consistent and interesting, and would give great advantage to late developers, poor mathematicians, and less able children. Decimals would be taught before fractions (the teaching of fractions would, in fact, be much reduced) and decimals would belong to the "real" world, not just to the school curriculum. Psychologically it is suggested that children would lose some of their resistance to mathematics, which is built up in the primary schools through the feeling that they are forced to learn "stupid" things such as the multiplication of two compound quantities (eg tons, cwt, qr, lb and £sd), and the manipulation of our cumbersome and illogical weights and measures.'

It is not altogether irrelevant to note that, as part of the same investigation, a series of tests were carried out to discover what effects might follow the introduction of decimal coinage. The tests covered problems in simple addition, multiplication, division, subtraction and conversion in £sd and decimals, the results being recorded for time and accuracy. A small office group showed a saving of time up to 30%, with errors reduced by approximately 50%, when using decimals. Tests were also made at two schools, and for children of an average age of 9 years 4 months, the time saved when using decimals was 40% and errors were also reduced by 40%. These tests of course related to money, but the difficulty in handling £sd is of precisely the same nature as that involved with yards, feet and inches, or any other series of the imperial family.

We can look at this from another angle by examining school textbooks of arithmetic. Many of these have now been revised to take account of the change to the metric system in schools, so that a direct comparison can be made between the old imperial and the new metric editions. In the earlier version of a typical textbook for 8-year-olds each separate quantity—length, weight, capacity—requires several pages of closely packed type; first a statement of the units, their ratios, the scales that may be encountered; then the inevitable compound arithmetic for each case: reduce 2 lb 10 oz to ounces, reduce 43 cwt to tons and hundredweights, add 3 lb 8 oz to 4 lb 6 oz, subtract 3 lb 13 oz from 4 lb 6 oz, multiply 1 ton 5 cwt by 5, divide 11 stone 4 lb by 3; share $1\frac{1}{4}$ lb of sweets between four boys and express the answer in ounces; each type of calculation repeated many times to afford sufficient practice. In the metric system all this is omitted, as it has already been dealt with once for all on a decimal basis. The whole treatment seems far and away more logical, less artificial; above all, it saves precious time.

A section at the end of the textbook provides a condensed account of the imperial system, and all the familiar key-signatures appear again: tables to be memorised, scales, reduction, compound arithmetic; they are unavoidable in the imperial system.

This question of children's education is of such immense importance that it is worth looking at another textbook of arithmetic, this time firmly wedded to the imperial system, but nevertheless reprinted within the last few years. It is for rather older children, and contains about 200 pages. The first 26 deal with the basic rules of whole-number arithmetic: addition, subtraction, multiplication, division (*see* Figure 5, page 37). The £sd system is then explained, and it is pointed out that the ordinary arithmetic just learned has to be drastically modified to deal with the intrusion of 12 and 20; the process of addition becomes 'compound addition', and so on, and a new process called 'reduction' is introduced: 'reduce 2137 pence to pounds, shillings and pence'. This section occupies 18 pages.

The book then tackles weights and measures, and tabulates all the units of weight, length, area, volume and capacity, after which it returns to compound arithmetic and reduction—the same general principles, but different sets of numbers for each quantity. (There are some magnificent collectors' specimens here, such as the reduction of 33 631 207 square inches to 5 acres, 1 rood, 25 sq yd, 6 sq ft, 115 sq in!) This part of the book extends to 15 pages. It is followed by 27 pages dealing with fractional

Figure 5

Analysis of Contents of an Arithmetic Book

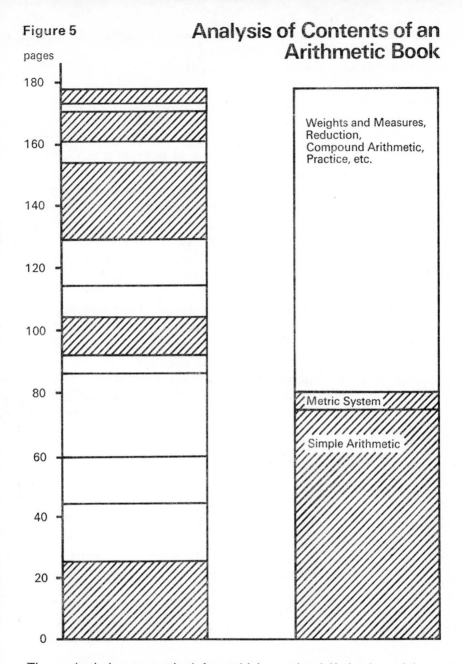

The unshaded areas on the left could be omitted if the imperial system were abandoned. They correspond to the upper block on the right-hand side.

arithmetic, which is included almost entirely to facilitate the handling of problems in weights and measures.

At this point decimals are introduced and occupy 18 pages, of which, however, six are concerned solely with the inter-conversion of decimals with fractions or weights-and-measures quantities. The process known as 'practice' is described in 10 pages, virtually all of which are concerned with its application to weights and measures. Proportion, percentages, interest, and stocks and shares occupy 40 pages, of which about 15 are concerned with weights and measures. Square roots and mensuration take 16 pages, including about six on weights and measures. Foreign decimal currency systems and the metric system are covered in a mere seven pages, and even so, two of them deal with conversion to our own units. This virtually concludes the book, and on taking stock it appears that, at a conservative estimate, no less than 97 pages—over half the book—could be dispensed with if imperial units were abandoned along with pounds, shillings and pence.

The treatment given to the metric system takes barely three pages. Nevertheless, it says practically all that needs to be said. The examples are, by comparison, extraordinarily simple: 'reduce 23.715 km to metres. Moving the decimal point three places gives 23 715 m'.

Nothing in this analysis is intended to be in any way a criticism of the book, which is excellent. The criticism is of the system on which it is based.

For those who have forgotten what school arithmetic is really like, the following actual examples are offered and compared with the equivalent

	Example A				Example B
	£				
	$13 \cdot 80$	= value of 1 ton			
$(\times 11)$	$151 \cdot 80$	= value of 11 tons			£$13 \cdot 58$
$(\times \frac{1}{5})$	$2 \cdot 76$	=	,,	,, 4 cwt	$\times 11 \cdot 51$
$(\times \frac{1}{2})$	$1 \cdot 38$	=	,,	,, 2 cwt	
$(\times \frac{1}{4})$	$0 \cdot 345$	=	,,	,, 2 qr	$135 \cdot 8$
$(\times \frac{1}{8})$	$0 \cdot 043$	=	,,	,, 7 lb	$13 \cdot 58$
$(\times \frac{1}{7})$	$0 \cdot 006$	=	,,	,, 1 lb	$6 \cdot 79$
					$0 \cdot 1358$
	$156 \cdot 334$ =		total		£$156 \cdot 31$ = total

ie £$156 \cdot 33$ to the nearest new penny.

Example *C*

```
        ton cwt   qr    lb    oz    ton  cwt   qr    lb    oz
127) 142    7    3     20    7  ( 1    2     1     19    9
     127

      15
        ×20
           300
           ───
           307
           254
           ───
            53
              ×4
              212
              ───
              215
              127
              ───
               88
                 ×28
                 1760
                  704
                  ───
                 2484
                 1270
                 ───
                 1214
                 1143
                 ───
                   71
                     ×16
                      710
                      426
                      ────
                     1143
                     1143
                     ────
```

Example *D*

```
127) 144 680.94 (1139.22
     127
     ───
     176
     127
     ───
      498
      381
      ───
     1170
     1143
     ───
       279
       254
       ───
        254
        254
        ───
```

calculations as they would be carried out in the metric system. The first is an application of 'practice'. 'Find the value of 11 tons 6 cwt 2 qr 8 lb at £13·80 per ton' (formerly of course £13.16.0 per ton). The working is set out as in Example *A*.

The metric equivalent is 'find the value of 11.51 tonne at £13·58 per tonne', and the working is as shown in Example *B*. This is just straightforward decimal arithmetic. The complete absence of the mental gymnastics associated with practice will be obvious. (The 2p difference arises from the rounding errors in conversion.)

The process of compound division is also very instructive as an indication of the complexities of the imperial system. Consider the following: 'divide 142 tons 7 cwt 3 qr 20 lb 7 oz by 127' (Example *C*).

The same calculation appears in metric terms as 'divide 144 680.94 kg by 127' (Example *D*). The saving in space alone is considerable, to say nothing of the reduction in mental effort.

The following extract from the Report of the Australian Senate Select Committee on the metric system affords an admirable summing-up of this section. 'Almost without exception, education authorities favour the early adoption of the metric system on the grounds that this would simplify and unify the teaching of mathematics and science, reduce errors, save teaching time and lead to a better understanding of basic mathematical principles' [*13*].

3
Advantages in Technical Use

The distinction between this section and the last is that we are now considering activities carried out only by certain limited sections of the populace, instead of directing our attention to matters of concern to almost everyone. We are, however, still concerned with matters involving comparatively large numbers of people; we shall leave to the next section still more highly specialised topics, such as scientific research and advanced design and development work. The present section includes commerce, engineering, and agriculture, which constitute a large proportion of the gross national product.

3.1 Metrication and the metric system

It is here that the confusion between the metric system and metrication is most acute. Many articles and letters which have been published under the general heading of metrication scarcely mention the metric system itself at all. To some in industry, metrication is seen as a golden opportunity for rationalisation, the adoption of international standards, simplification of nomenclature and so on. To others, metrication means changing to new standard sizes, re-tooling, new screw threads, etc.—expensive matters which may seem to offer no particular advantage, together with the prospect of having to make and store both imperial and metric versions for many years to cope with the continued demand for spare parts. Neither group is in fact very much concerned with the metric system itself. This confusion was encountered in the British Association enquiry in 1960, as the following extract shows: 'In view of the great importance of the effects

41

(of changing standards, etc.) which a change to the metric system within the engineering industry would have, it is not surprising that many of those who are most aware of these effects tend to regard them as dominating the whole question. On the other hand, a great many people concerned with fields of industry and commerce unrelated to engineering have little appreciation of the importance or complexity of problems of standardisation. The varying degree of awareness of some of the major effects of complete adoption of the metric system tended to confuse our enquiry. It is likely that different respondents have interpreted "adoption" in different ways, and this affects the validity of our enquiries about costs and benefits' [12]. In view of this widespread misunderstanding it may be as well to reiterate that the present study is concerned solely with the metric system itself, and not with possible consequential developments of the kind just mentioned.

The difference between everyday and technical usage, as the terms are interpreted here, is one of degree rather than kind. The same units are involved, and are used in much the same way, but in technical affairs transactions involving units are much more frequent, the quantities involved are often greater, the records are bulkier, and calculations are more commonplace. To a considerable extent therefore the arguments that were advanced in the previous section apply here also, often with greatly added force, and we shall find ourselves treading familiar ground. It will accordingly be unnecessary to repeat the discussion about the availability of units of convenient size, and the superiority of nomenclature, abbreviations and scales which distinguish the metric system, except to emphasise their increased importance. The argument will now be concerned more with the greater convenience of calculation, and to a lesser extent with the greater compactness and flexibility of quantity statements in the metric system.

3.2 The arithmetic of imperial units

It will be helpful to start with some general remarks about the way in which the imperial system and its associated compound arithmetic lead to an increase in the amount of work entailed in calculations. The effect depends almost entirely on the use of two or more units for a given quantity, and this is often associated with the degree of precision required. Consider, for example, the following calculation: a field of 27 acres is bought for £2000; what is the proportionate value of a plot of 5 acres? The answer is simply £2000 × 5 ÷ 27: a matter of basic, unavoidable arithmetic. In metric terms of similar precision the areas might be given as 11 hectares and 2 hectares respectively, leading to a value of £2000 × 2 ÷ 11; the arithmetic is just the same. Suppose, however, that a greater degree of precision is demanded, and that accordingly the areas are quoted as 26 acres 3 roods and 5 acres 1 rood; at once we are faced with an extra step of reduction before the calculation proper can start: 26 × 4 + 3 = 107 roods, 5 × 4 + 1 = 21 roods, leading to £2000 × 21 ÷ 107. In metric terms the extra precision is achieved merely by adding a decimal place: the areas are now given as 10.7 ha and 2.1 ha, and the calculation is £2000 × 2.1 ÷ 10.7 without any preamble. Still higher precision is seldom required, but makes the point with even greater force: if the two areas were quoted as 26 acres 2 roods 975 sq yd and 5 acres 1 rood 35 sq yd, the result would be a calculation of considerable complexity and labour. In metric language we should just add one more decimal place, and proceed as before with scarcely any increase in the amount of work required. To give another example, finding the total weight of six articles each weighing 2 lb requires no more nor less effort than if they weighed 2 kg; but compare 6 times 2 lb 7 oz with 6 times 2.15 kg. The latter is still utterly simple, but the former requires an additional division of 42 by 16.

A second source of unnecessary arithmetic lies in the difficulty we experience in appreciating the significance of very large and very small numbers—one of the formative factors, as we have seen, in the development of unit systems. Suppose it is decided to divide a field of 2 acres into 100 equal plots; the area of each plot can be written down at once as 0.02 or $\frac{1}{50}$ acre, but neither expression conveys any clear idea as to its size. We have to convert to square yards, writing 2 × 4840 ÷ 100 = 96.8 sq yd, which we may visualize as about 8 yards by 12, and not till then do we begin to get a 'feel' of the matter. Similarly, if we have 10 000 castings each weighing 3 ounces, the total weight is obviously 30 000 oz, but this conveys no real idea of the magnitude of the load until we go through a process of unit-conversion, dividing by 16 and 112 to change the unit and obtain a number of manageable size. Exactly the same considerations arise when we are using the metric system, but since the ratios between units are always based on ten no increase in the amount of arithmetic is entailed. If a 2 hectare field is divided into 100 plots, each one is of area 0.02 ha = 200 square metres, ie perhaps 20 m × 10 m; if each casting weighs 80 grammes, then 10 000 weigh 800 000 grammes = 800 kg = 0.8 tonne; the quantities spring into intelligible form with no effort at all.

A third way in which inter-unit ratios appear results from the fact that

43

convenience, or sometimes merely convention, causes different sectors of commerce and technology to make a different choice of unit where there is more than one that might be regarded as equally suitable. Some people work in yards and others in feet; some use seconds and others minutes. As soon as the two differing usages come together for any reason a conversion has to take place before progress can be made, and the non-decimal ratio produces its inevitable ration of arithmetic.

Examples of all these situations will be given in this section.

3.3 Units in the commercial world

We start by considering commerce, that is the buying and selling of goods but not their manufacture. The basic applications of units are in the estimation and specification of quantities, and the calculation of costs. The people concerned may be assumed to be competent in arithmetic, and the availability of calculating machines and other aids to computation is much more a factor to be reckoned with. These considerations point unmistakably to the advantages of a decimal system of weights and measures. There is no need to go to textbook examples to demonstrate the awkwardness of imperial units for computations of any size. Consider, for example, a straightforward addition in weight units, perhaps to ascertain the total sales over a week (example A):

Example A				Example B			Example C
ton	cwt	qr	lb	cwt	lb		kg
	3	2	23	3	79		188.0
	5	3	12	5	96	112)315(2	297.5
	11	2	17	11	73	224	592.0
	4	1	14	4	42	—	222.5
	3	0	25	3	25	91	163.5
1	8	3	7	28	91		1463.5

First, we add up the pounds column to get 91, which we divide by 28, by not too simple mental arithmetic, to obtain 3 qr and a remainder of 7 lb. Next we add the quarters column to get 11, which we divide by 4 to convert to 2 cwt and 3 qr; the hundredweights column adds up to 28, which we interpret as 1 ton 8 cwt. The essential additions, which use ordinary decimal arithmetic, are interrupted by a series of unit conversions, each involving a different division.

44

One simplification of this procedure would be to eliminate the quarter, whose ratio to the hundredweight is only 1 : 4 (but strictly speaking, we should have been using the stone as well!); we may therefore consider the calculation again without it (Example *B*). Here one unit conversion is left out, but we are faced with an awkward division by 112 in order to move to the hundredweight column. Another defect of this procedure is the appearance of 91 lb in the answer, which would probably not be regarded as acceptable.

The same calculation in metric terms, using straightforward decimal arithmetic throughout, is shown in example *C*. The figures speak for themselves; the non-decimal relations between the imperial units add quite substantially to the work of almost every calculation. They also take up more room, and make the use of non-specialised calculating machines difficult.

In some organisations a degree of simplification is introduced by working entirely in decimals of one selected unit, for example the hundredweight. The first entry, 3 cwt 2 qr 23 lb, would be converted to 3.705 cwt, and so on. The arithmetic is then the same as when using metric units, but there are still two serious limitations to the utility of this procedure. First, all quantities have to be reduced to the chosen unit before the calculation can begin, and the final answer of 28.812 cwt has to be converted back again, because decimals of a hundredweight are not generally understood. Secondly, there is no likelihood of a general agreement as to which unit to choose; the hundredweight is suitable for the example just given, but would be quite inappropriate for an example involving smaller quantities expressed largely in pounds and ounces. Such procedures are therefore almost always 'private' ones, restricted to particular firms. Once again, the metric system provides complete freedom in this respect, since changes from one unit to another merely entail the moving of a decimal point. Efforts to make the imperial system less troublesome are nearly always steps along the road to a completely decimalised system.

Probably the commonest calculation in commerce is the multiplication of a quantity by a price per unit quantity, for example, to find a buying or selling price, a freightage or storage charge, a customs due, and so on. Some of the sting of such calculations has been drawn with the introduction of decimal currency, and we may now congratulate ourselves at the disappearance of horrors such as reckoning the cost of 3 tons 5 cwt 2 qr 5 lb of mercury at £1 3*s* 7*d* a pound; but we have still one more step to take before we attain the ultimate simplicity of 3329.8 kg at £2·60 a kilogramme—done in a moment on a calculating machine.

Finally, the much greater compactness of metric statements is a great advantage in commerce, where many thousands of quantities are recorded daily. With the aid of the decimal point and the decimal relations between units there is never any need to write the name of more than one unit, or to use more than one column. The statement 4376.152 kg is perfectly clear and unambiguous, and far more concise than the imperial counterpart 4 tons 6 cwt 0 qr 15 lb 12$\frac{1}{4}$ oz. The saving in paper, clerical work, and so on is obvious.

The discussion has so far been concerned with comparatively large-scale commercial transactions, but the work of the retail shopkeeper should not be overlooked. Ordering, stocktaking and invoicing all involve units, and even though the quantities may be smaller the total effort is still considerable. Unlike the householder who shirks the accurate calculation of an area, the shopkeeper cannot shrug off such a task. He cannot even get away with a rough approximation. If he sells a fitted carpet 14 ft 3 in by 9 ft 8 in at £2·30 a square yard, with a surcharge of 10% for cutting, etc., he must be prepared to work out the price to the nearest penny or so. He will probably use 'practice', or he may obtain assistance from some sort of ready-reckoner, a tabulated collection of results of similar calculations. Whatever the method he does it quickly and efficiently—it is after all his job. But how unnecessary given the same problem in metric terms. 4.35 m by 2.95 m at £2·70 per square metre, plus 10%, becomes a matter of straightforward decimal arithmetic: 4.35 × 2.95 × 2.70 × 1.10, quite easily worked out longhand if necessary, or, more probably, on a calculating machine.

An engineer's slide-rule will give the answer to an accuracy of about a quarter per cent, which is four times better than a penny in the pound and adequate for many purposes. It should be noted that these aids to computation—the slide rule and the calculating machine—depend on decimals. They are of no help with imperial units. It would, of course, be possible to construct calculating machines for feet and inches, pounds and ounces, or gallons and pints, but a different machine would be required for each pair. In the metric system *all* units are on a decimal scale, in line with decimal currency and our ordinary way of counting, and one calculating machine serves for all purposes.

3.4 Technical calculations

In many other aspects of technical usage the superiority of the metric system lies primarily in its simplification of calculations, and a series of examples will be given from a variety of spheres. We start with two having an agricultural flavour. The first is to determine the amount of fertiliser required to treat a field of $6\frac{1}{4}$ acres at a rate of 2 ounces a square yard. Since an acre is 4840 square yards, the necessary quantity is $6\frac{1}{4} \times 4840 \times 2$ oz $= 60\,500$ oz. This is too large a figure to be appreciated, so we divide by 16 to get 3781 lb and then by 112 to get $33\frac{3}{4}$ cwt. Notice that the real calculation here is just an area times a weight per unit area, that is the multiplication of two quantities only; but other figures, 4840, 16 and 112, have crept in to add to the labour and create additional opportunities for arithmetical error. In metric terms we might have a field of $2\frac{1}{2}$ hectares and a dosage of 60 grammes per square metre; since a hectare $= 10\,000$ square metres, the required quantity is $25\,000 \times 60$ g $= 1\,500\,000$ g, or 1.5 tonnes. The calculation has been reduced to the single essential multiplication together with the movement of the decimal point.

The complexity of 'imperial arithmetic' leads to attempts at simplification through the use of fractions and 'cancelling'. We might write $6\frac{1}{4} = \frac{25}{4}$, so that the quantity is

$$\frac{25}{4} \times \frac{\overset{605}{\cancel{4840}}}{\cancel{16}} \times \frac{\cancel{2}}{112} = \frac{25 \times 605}{448}$$

This leaves us not much better off.

The second example is to calculate the number of gallons of water represented by a rainfall of $1\frac{1}{4}$ inches on a catchment area of 37 square miles. In cubic inches the volume of water is $1.25 \times 37 \times (1760 \times 36)^2 = 185\,670$ million; so that the amount in gallons is found by dividing by 277.42 cubic inches per gallon, and equals $669\frac{1}{4}$ million gallons. In metric terms we might have a rainfall of 3.1 cm on an area of 96 sq km; working in metres, the volume is $0.031 \times 96 \times 1\,000\,000$ cubic metres, $= 2.98$ million cu m; this would probably be an acceptable statement as it stands, but conversion to litres would merely require multiplication by 1000. Note the intrusion of 1760 and 36, both twice, into the imperial calculation, together with the obnoxious 277.42; five arithmetic operations instead of one. (As a matter of interest, a rainfall of 1 cm on 1 hectare represents 0.01 m $\times 10\,000$ m$^2 = 100$ cubic metres, which weighs 100 tonnes.)

Closely related to this example is an architect's calculation of the weight of water represented by a layer 2 inches deep on a flat roof 24 ft 6 in by 30 ft 4 in. Converting to inches we have a total volume of $294 \times 364 \times 2$

cubic inches (already we have had to do a little mental arithmetic); then a handbook tells us that a cubic foot of water weighs 62.3 lb, so the required weight is $(294 \times 364 \times \frac{2}{1728}) \times 62.3$ lb $= 7716$ lb, which we might wish to convert into tons, hundredweights and so on. In metric terms we could have a layer 5 cm deep on a roof 7.5 m by 9.2 m, giving a total volume of $7.5 \text{ m} \times 9.2 \text{ m} \times 0.05 \text{ m} = 3.45$ cubic metres; and since a cubic metre of water weighs 1000 kg the total weight is 3450 kg or 3.45 tonnes. Once again it should be noted that the metric working is entirely free from numbers other than those essential to the problem.

Another example is that of determining the amount of asphalt required to provide a layer $1\frac{1}{2}$ inches thick on a path 4 ft 10 in wide and 1 mile ç furlongs in length. Mental arithmetic enables us to work in terms of yards, and the required amount is $\frac{1}{24} \times \frac{11}{8} \times 1760 \times \frac{58}{36}$ cubic yards. In metric terms we might have a layer 4 cm thick on a path 158 cm wide and 2.2 km long; the amount is then $0.04 \times 1.58 \times 2200$ cubic metres; three figures to manipulate instead of seven; two multiplications only instead of three multiplications and three divisions, and no pre-reduction needed.

These examples have involved, in essence, only addition and multiplication; division tells the same story. Suppose it is desired to build a wall 20 yards long, 10 feet high and 18 inches thick, from concrete blocks 18 in $\times$ 9 in $\times$ 6 in; approximately how many will be needed, allowing 5% for mortar? In order to divide we must reduce all the quantities to the same units; here the inch seems likely to be the most convenient. The total volume of the wall, less mortar, is $(20 \times 3 \times 12) \times (10 \times 12) \times 18 \times 0.95$, and the volume of a single block is $18 \times 9 \times 6$, both in cubic inches, so the required number is found by dividing one expression by the other.

Alternatively, suppose the wall is 20 metres long, 3 metres high and 50 centimetres thick, and that the blocks measure 50 cm $\times$ 25 cm $\times$ 12 cm; then working in centimetres the number of blocks will be $(2000 \times 300 \times 50 \times 0.95) \div (50 \times 25 \times 12)$. The imperial working involves ten numbers, the metric only the essential seven. In this sort of calculation the amount of work can sometimes be reduced by cancelling, but this process can of course be applied with the metric system as well, and in any case the figures are not always helpful. Consider this even simpler example: how many castings each weighing 1 lb $3\frac{1}{2}$ oz can be obtained from 2 tons of metal? Again, the essential division must be prefaced by reduction to a common unit, and the full calculation is $(2 \times 2240 \times 16) \div (16 + 3\frac{1}{2})$.

If the weights were 550 grammes and 2 tonnes the number would be $2\,000\,000 \div 550$; two figures instead of five; one operation instead of four.

It would be simple to give endless examples demonstrating the superiority of the metric system in any but the very simplest of calculations, but mere repetition would be tedious and unhelpful. The following examples have been included in order to illustrate additional aspects of the matter. Suppose we have a tank, measuring 3 ft $\times$ 1 ft 9 in $\times$ 1 ft 6 in, and we wish to know how many gallons of water it will hold. We put $3 \times 1\frac{3}{4} \times 1\frac{1}{2} = 3 \times \frac{7}{4} \times \frac{3}{2} = \frac{63}{8}$ cubic feet, and then multiply by 6.23, the number of gallons in a cubic foot, to obtain 49 gallons. The metric equivalent might be a tank 1 m $\times$ 0.7 m $\times$ 0.5 m $= 0.35$ cubic metres, and since a cubic metre equals 1000 litres the capacity is 350 litres; a far simpler calculation. This example stresses the awkwardness of the gallon. It was originally introduced as the volume of water which weighs ten pounds and is not without its advantages as a result of this link, but it has had most unfortunate consequences in other types of calculation.

Next consider the preparation of a fuel mixture for a two-stroke engine. Suppose we are instructed to add oil to petrol in the proportion of $1:50$, and that we have a can containing 4 gallons of petrol; how much oil should we add? Since 4 gallons equals 32 pints we need $\frac{32}{50}$ or $\frac{16}{25}$ pints of oil; our measuring vessel, however, will be graduated in fluid ounces ($\frac{1}{20}$ pint) so we require $(\frac{16}{25}) \times 20 = \frac{64}{5}$, ie approximately 13 fl oz. If we were using metric units, with say 20 litres of petrol, we should need $\frac{20}{50} = 0.4$ litre $= 400$ millilitres of oil, and we should have no difficulty in measuring out this quantity in a litre measure graduated in 100 ml steps. Note the almost complete absence of anything deserving the name of arithmetic.

Finally, consider the situation where careful measurements have been taken of an armchair in order to make a loose cover, using feet, inches and fractions of an inch, and it is decided to add 1% to allow for possible shrinkage. This would present us with a most vexatious little calculation. It is child's play when the measurements are in metric units, because 1% can be found merely by shifting a decimal point; 1% of 1.234 m is 0.012 m or 12 mm.

3.5 Some consequences of the imperial system

It has already been pointed out that the great variety of imperial units available can be a positive disadvantage at times. In many branches of engineering, a load will be quoted in tons in one set of circumstances and in pounds in another; both figures will be in decimals, but sooner or later 2240 will appear to add its quota to the arithmetic. Again, in air-conditioning calculations one has to take account of the comparatively small amounts of water-vapour contained in atmospheric air, and the convention is to measure the air in pounds and the water-vapour in grains. This is a convenient arrangement as far as it goes because both figures are then of reasonable size: for example, a pound of air might contain 50 grains of water-vapour. In due course, however, grains have to be converted to pounds and the remarkable figure of 7000 intrudes itself into the calculation. In both these examples the metric system offers the benefits of units of convenient size without the penalty of awkward conversion factors. In the air-conditioning example, for instance, the weight of air could be given in kilogrammes and that of vapour in grammes.

The compound arithmetic which results from even the simplest calculation in terms of feet, inches and fractions has led to a very interesting development in the carpentry and associated trades: an ingenious duo-decimal arithmetic for calculating areas and volumes. The foot is divided into twelve inches as usual, but the inch is divided into 12 'parts' and the part into twelve 'thirds'; the same process is applied to square measure and to cubic measure. Calculations can then proceed as in ordinary arithmetic, but with twelves instead of tens. The immediate effect is a considerable simplification of the arithmetic, but some unit conversion is ultimately necessary because a 'part' and a 'third' of a square or cubic foot are not recognisable by those unaccustomed to the system, and they have to be expressed in more familiar units; for example a 'third' of a cubic foot is $\frac{1}{144}$ cu ft = 12 cu in. The emergence of this special form of arithmetic, with its own peculiar nomenclature and symbols, clearly shows that the advantages of having units related by a common factor have long been apparent even to people entirely wedded to imperial units. When using the metric system all the advantages are obtained without any need for such special devices, and the results are immediately intelligible to everyone.

It is also pertinent to remark that the predominance of the metric system in the rest of the world means that we have to carry a massive load of conversion between imperial and metric units, a far greater handicap to the few countries still using the imperial system than to the majority using the metric system. This important consideration is, strictly speaking, outside the scope of this study, since it does not concern—except indirectly—the relative merits of the two systems. Nevertheless, it will be instructive to give a simple example showing the kind of situation that arises repeatedly because of the predominance of the metric system. A small business requires 500 gallons of a certain liquid chemical, and the purchasing officer wishes to find out the cost. The catalogue quotes the price as £130 a ton. He must therefore find the weight of 500 gallons, and to do this he needs to know the density of the liquid. On consulting a handbook of physical data he finds that the density is given as 0.87 gramme per millilitre. He is, therefore, faced with more arithmetic in order to reconcile the units. He ascertains that a gallon is equal to 4546 millilitres, and that a gramme equals $\frac{1}{453\cdot6}$ pound, so that he can now calculate the weight in pounds; since the price is in terms of the ton a further unit conversion is needed, and the final answer is

$$£\frac{500 \times 4546 \times 0.87 \times 130}{453\cdot6 \times 2240} = £253\cdot01$$

It will be observed that the original problem involved only three numbers, but that two more—4546 and 453·6—have intruded themselves because of the confusion of units, and the imperial system has contributed 2240 as well. These complications are avoided altogether when using metric units throughout.

3.6 Units in engineering production

In the very important sphere of engineering production, design work may involve carrying out complex calculations relating to stresses and so on. For most people engaged on production, however, the units of length are almost the only ones to be used and calculation is limited to very simple operations. Here we find the draughtsman producing the dimensioned drawing which conveys instructions to the artisan in the workshop, who in turn reads the drawing and sets his lathe or other machine tool to produce the required component. Both are concerned almost exclusively with the size of the component and make little or no use of any other units.

In much general engineering there is a deeply rooted tradition in this country of working in 'binary' fractions of an inch; $\frac{1}{2}, \frac{1}{4}, \frac{1}{8}, \frac{1}{16}, \frac{1}{32}, \frac{1}{64}$. Although long practice renders the British workman highly skilled in handling these fractions, experience shows clearly that the use of decimals which accompanies the adoption of the metric system is both quicker and less liable to error. The greater ease of reading from a decimal scale will be examined in detail in the next sub-section. The greater brevity and clarity of metric expressions are also worth re-emphasising. In the following sets of figures, dimensions are given in both imperial and metric terms, to about the same degree of precision. The first has a precision of half-an-inch, such as might be used by a builder for rough work; the metric dimensions are given in centimetres. Note that the foot is introduced in the imperial statement; this is conventional for lengths over 23 inches (though practice varies).

70 cm	2 ft $3\frac{1}{2}$ in
71 cm	2 ft 4 in
72 cm	2 ft $4\frac{1}{2}$ in
73 cm	2 ft $4\frac{1}{2}$ in
74 cm	2 ft 5 in
75 cm	2 ft $5\frac{1}{2}$ in

The two-figure metric statements are obviously far more compact; they can cover a range from zero to 99 cm, ie approximately $3\frac{1}{4}$ ft. Adding a third figure and working in millimetres covers the same range with a ten-fold increase in precision (1 mm $= \frac{1}{32}$ in approximately) but requires the use of still more complicated fractions of an inch:

700 mm	2 ft $3\frac{9}{16}$ in
701 mm	2 ft $3\frac{19}{32}$ in
702 mm	2 ft $3\frac{5}{8}$ in
703 mm	2 ft $3\frac{11}{16}$ in
704 mm	2 ft $3\frac{23}{32}$ in
705 mm	2 ft $3\frac{3}{4}$ in

The imperial expressions are not only much longer but take up more room in the other direction as well, a distinct disadvantage on a complicated drawing.

The fractional expressions are more difficult to read because of the varying denominator, and this adds noticeably to the fatigue of studying drawings. Comparisons, too, are very troublesome, for the same reason: to judge whether $\frac{29}{64}$ is greater or less than $\frac{7}{16}$ entails a distinct mental effort, whereas comparing 11.5 mm and 11.1 mm gives no trouble at all.

Most design calculations, whether or not they require great precision, are carried out in decimals because it is so much simpler. Nevertheless, the results are frequently converted into fractions or other units before being passed to the workshop for manufacture: for example, one finds such phrases as '. . . 2.28 in, say $2\frac{1}{4}$ in' or '. . . 6.45 ft, say 6 ft 6 in'. With metric units there is no need for this sort of thing. When, as is sometimes the case, the actual calculations are carried out in terms of fractional expressions, the difficulties are very considerable, and the speed with which the experienced man can work should not blind us to the essential inefficiency of the procedure. Consider the following example (taken from an American journal): a design checker has to add a series of lengths of components together, to ensure that the overall size is correct; they are given as 2 ft 1 in + 5 ft 10 in + 3 ft $9\frac{5}{8}$ in + 1 ft $5\frac{3}{4}$ in + 0 ft $8\frac{1}{2}$ in + 6 ft $5\frac{7}{8}$ in. One has only to time oneself doing this sum, as against the metric equivalent $0.635 + 1.778 + 1.158 + 0.451 + 0.216 + 1.978$ metres, to appreciate the point. Some people who constantly have to manipulate fractions actually find it simpler to memorise the decimal equivalents and use them instead.

The use of fractions is scarcely ever extended to finer limits than the sixty-fourth of an inch, and this is far from sufficient for 'precision' work. From the time of Whitworth, that is for well over a hundred years, precision workers in this country have used the decimalised inch. A typical dimension might be quoted as $23.065 \, {}^{+0.005}_{-0.001}$ inches, meaning that the length of the part produced must lie between 23.070 and 23.064 inches. The last decimal place, representing one-thousandth of an inch, is a familiar and well-appreciated magnitude to the workman, and represents the limit of accuracy for a great deal of work, though higher accuracies— even to a millionth of an inch—are by no means rare. It will be obvious that, by working with a single unit only, which is decimally subdivided, two essential features of the metric system have been adopted, so that no significant difference can be expected when comparing the metric system in the same context. Many draughtsmen and craftsmen in this country have accustomed themselves to working with both with equal facility. In the metric system it is usual to use the millimetre as the basic unit, and as this is only about $\frac{1}{25}$ inch the figures look a little different: the example just quoted would appear as $585.85 \, {}^{+0.12}_{-0.02}$ mm, but essentially there is no alteration in procedure.

It is intriguing to note that, even when working entirely in decimals, the British craftsman retains a predilection for fractions. Small tools such as drills, and components such as nuts and bolts, are made in a range of standard sizes, which are normally expressed in fractions of an inch. As a result, many of the decimal figures which appear on an engineering drawing may, on closer inspection, prove to be fractions re-expressed as decimals. The same attitude is extended to the coarser tolerances. The use of millimetres releases the mind from this preoccupation and leads to a small but useful simplification. Designers frequently tot up lists of

53

tolerances to find the average, and even this little exercise in decimal arithmetic is made slightly easier when they are expressed in millimetres, because of the abandonment of fraction-equivalents.

For work of the highest precision in the metric system use may be made of the micrometre (micron), which equals 0.000 04 inch approximately, and this has a slight advantage over the inch as it avoids having to write five places of decimals. On the whole, there is very little difference between working with inches and millimetres in the sphere of precision engineering.

In view of the emphasis in this section on calculations, it may be as well to repeat that this is not the only aspect of technical usage in which the metric system has something to offer.

3.7 Scales of measurement

Attention has already been drawn to the wide variety of scales associated with the imperial system, and the assertion has been made that the single decimal scale of the metric system is essentially more efficient. This claim will now be examined in greater detail, with particular reference to the 'binary' scale used in measuring length and certain other quantities. A binary scale is constructed by successively subdividing each interval by two, producing halves, quarters, eighths, sixteenths, and so on. This is a very simple and easily understood procedure, but unfortunately it does not correspond with our choice of ten as the basis of expressing numbers. The awkward consequences emerge more and more clearly as one seeks to attain expressions of greater precision.

A scale used for measuring length directly is peculiar among scales in that its subdivisions are uniquely determined by the units used; two graduations whose distance apart is supposed to represent an inch must in fact be exactly an inch apart. Other scales are no more than analogues, and can be made to any convenient size provided they are properly calibrated. We start therefore by comparing scales of arbitrary length graduated into eighths and tenths (*see* Figure 6, page 55). The essential operation in using such a scale for rough work is to decide which graduation is nearest to the indicating arrow, and then to note the number of this graduation, counting from the left. In each scale the central graduation is accentuated to assist the eye. On the tenths scale (A) the number indicated is clearly 7, and we can write 0.7 at once. On the eighths scale (B) the number of the nearest graduation is 5, and we can write $\frac{5}{8}$ at once. There is scarcely any difference between these two operations, but had the number on the eighths scale been 6 we should undoubtedly have written $\frac{3}{4}$, and

Figure 6

Comparison of Binary and Decimal Scales

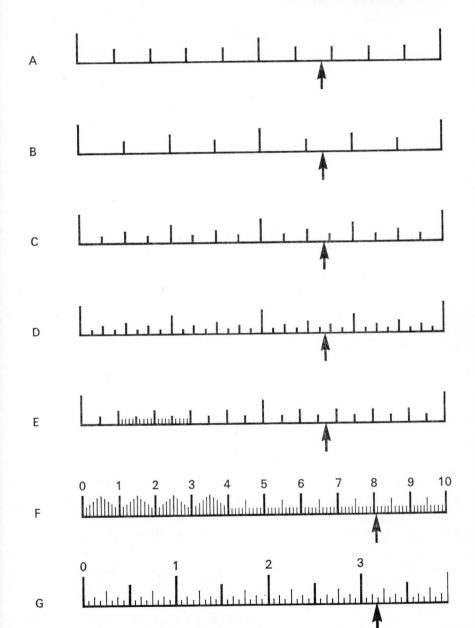

partly for this reason the eighths scale is constructed with the quarter marks accentuated as well as the halves. Thus an element of complexity creeps in even at this level.

Greater precision is obtained on the binary scale by dividing the eighths into sixteenths. The readings may now be expressed in halves, quarters, eighths and sixteenths, and the scale becomes correspondingly more complex. In the example (C) the practised eye might regard the nearest graduation to the arrow as 'three beyond the half' or perhaps 'one beyond five-eighths', following this by a fragment of mental arithmetic:

$$\tfrac{1}{2} = \tfrac{8}{16}, + 3 = \tfrac{11}{16}; \text{ or } \tfrac{5}{8} = \tfrac{10}{16}, + 1 = \tfrac{11}{16}.$$

Still greater precision requires the use of 32nds or 64ths. Scales are not often divided beyond 32nds, but estimation to 64ths is usually quite simple. The difficulty lies in assigning the right number to the graduation indicated. In example D the arrow lies between two 32nd graduations and therefore indicates a 64th, but it is far from obvious which one it is; counting up from the left is much too tedious a procedure. One method is to count in convenient blocks, such as $\tfrac{1}{2}+\tfrac{1}{8}+\tfrac{3}{64} = \tfrac{(32+8+3)}{64} = \tfrac{43}{64}$. Not until this process has been completed are we in a position to write anything down. The fact that a skilled man can read off $\tfrac{43}{64}$ at a glance should not be allowed to conceal the essential difficulty of the operation and the long practice needed to arrive at speed and reliability.

Reverting to the tenths scale (A), greater precision is achieved by adding a second place of decimals. Working across from the left we can at once write down 0.6 as the first step, and our minds are free to concentrate on the second figure. We imagine the space between 0.6 and 0.7 to be divided into ten parts, and since we never have to consider any other type of scale when using the metric system we quickly acquire the ability to estimate the next figure with accuracy; in the example, 7 appears to be appropriate, and we can add this to what we have already written down to obtain the final 0.67. Very little practice is needed to obtain an accuracy of two hundredths, which approaches the precision of one sixty-fourth, but we are using a far simpler scale and can work much more quickly. By putting in further graduations at $\tfrac{1}{20}$ intervals (scale E) the eye can be assisted to achieve a precision of $\tfrac{1}{100}$ without difficulty. If the scale is large enough the 100ths can be indicated, and the whole decimal scale is then repeated at $\tfrac{1}{10}$ the size (scale E); one can then begin to think about estimating yet another place of decimals, in precisely the same manner.

The comparative slowness of the binary scale can be effectively demonstrated by timing one's efforts to locate, on scales of equal size, values such as $\frac{27}{32}$ and $\frac{19}{64}$, in comparison with 0.79 or 0.37. The distinguishing feature of the decimal scale is that it corresponds to our decimal numbering system, so that precision can be attained in stages, each figure being separately determined on a scale of standard type which we can learn to use with speed and accuracy.

In measuring length, the change to the metric system implies not only replacing the binary scale by the decimal scale but altering the actual size of the unit. Typical metric and inch scales are shown as scales F and G. On the metric scale the eye quickly registers successively 8, 0 and 6, the last figure being estimated; this can be written down as 8.06 cm or 80.6 mm. It is found that a precision of about a quarter of a millimetre can readily be attained, and this corresponds to about a hundredth of an inch.

It is thought by many craftsmen that, for work not requiring the highest precision, the millimetre is more convenient than either the sixteenth of an inch, which is rather large and suitable only for coarse work, and the thirty-second, which is rather too fine for an ordinary wooden scale. The millimetre lies between the two, and has the further advantage that it can be used as the basic unit so that quantities can be expressed in terms of whole numbers. Some find it convenient to use a millimetre scale in which the length of the graduations is progressively varied to form a regular pattern (scale F). For work of greater precision the eye must be assisted by devices such as the vernier, and these are all used with decimal scales.

Draughtsmen frequently have to prepare drawings smaller than the objects they represent, and they customarily use special 'compressed' scales such that, for example, graduations which are actually $\frac{1}{2}$ inch apart are labelled as if they were 1 foot apart, the intervening spaces being subdivided into 12 'inches'. This practice produces a further great variety of scales which have to be mastered. When using the metric system the same practice can be followed but reductions of 1 in 10, 1 in 100, etc., result in scales of identical appearance (and indeed some draughtsmen do not bother to use special ones). Scales for the intermediate ratios of 1 in 2, 1 in 5, 1 in 20, etc., can be made to look very similar to the standard decimal scale and are quite easy to use.

Somewhat similar considerations arise in map-making. The popular 'one inch to a mile' maps are very convenient because of our familiarity with both inches and miles, but for technical purposes the representative fraction (RF) of 1/63 360 which this implies is a source of unnecessary arithmetic, particularly when calculating areas. Metric maps are made with RFs of 1/50 000, 1/100 000 and so on and are consequently much simpler technically; nevertheless the advantage to the general public is not lost because, for example, 1/50 000 is equivalent to 2 centimetres to the kilometre, a very simple and convenient relation.

3.8 Units in other industries

There are at least two branches of industry where the metric system has already made considerable headway. Electrical engineering, as we have seen, is based on a branch of science which developed after the metric system had been invented, and has always used metric units for the electrical aspects of its work, but it does not normally carry this over into the area of manufacture: the basic concept of a dynamo or motor will be worked out in metric units, but the final dimensions will be put on the drawing-board in inches. A certain amount of unit-conversion is therefore almost always involved, and could be avoided if the whole process of design were carried out in metric units. Electrical engineers often have to use peculiar, mixed units, part metric and part imperial, such as the watt per square inch. They are among the first to express their relief when they can use metric units throughout.

Pharmacy is another industry where the metric system has made substantial progress, though for completely different reasons. Pharmacy was an exceedingly ancient and esoteric art, and accordingly built up its own peculiar set of units for weight and capacity—the so-called apothecaries' measures: grain $\times 20 =$ scruple, $\times 3 =$ drachm, $\times 8 =$ ounce; minim $\times 60 =$ fluid drachm, $\times 8 =$ fluid ounce. It is many years since the pitfalls of this practice became obvious—misunderstandings and errors in a subject where mistakes could be highly dangerous. As long ago as 1878 the metric system was officially adopted by the American Marine Hospital Service, and in this country the General Medical Council was urging a change to metric units in 1904. Within recent years the increasing impact of science on medicine has given added momentum to the general movement, and the Weights and Measures Act of 1963 provided that the apothecaries' measure for trade purposes should cease to be lawful after a date which the Board of Trade might appoint. 1 January 1971 was the date appointed by order. The metric system is now extensively employed in pharmacies and hospitals and its use by medical practitioners is increasing.

Since units play almost as important a part in our lives as language itself, it is not surprising that a great deal has been said and written about the metric system as it has progressively supplanted older systems. Most of these observations have been concerned with its effects on commerce and industry, and are therefore appropriately considered in this section.

The proportion of fact, as distinct from opinion, is unfortunately rather small, and few serious attempts appear to have been made to assess the advantages of the metric system in a quantitative manner. The scientist regards its superiority as rather obvious, and is not interested in proving what appears to be self-evident. The original metric countries might perhaps have been expected to do something on these lines, but for the last hundred years or so the system has been so completely accepted by them that it has not been regarded as a matter worth discussing. The non-metric countries have debated its proposed adoption over and over again, but to a great extent the argument has been concerned with the cost and inconvenience of the change rather than the merits of the rival systems; indeed, for many years even the stoutest opponents of the metric system have been inclined to start their argument by admitting that 'it is a better system, but . . .'. Useful material can be found in some of the early debates, but if one goes back too far one has to remember that the metric system was then being compared with the appalling hotch-potch of units which it was replacing in different parts of Europe.

Nevertheless, here and there remarks stand out, telling as much in a few words as a page of argument or worked examples: the vigorous, forthright opinions of people who have experienced both the metric system and our own and have no doubt where their preference lies. As far back as 1853 one may discern the emergence of strong preferences for the metric system [9], among those concerned with trade, engineering and science, and similar opinions may be found cropping up at intervals thereafter [14, 15, 16, 17, 18].

It may be argued that nothing is easier than to pick out all the favourable comments from a great volume of mixed evidence, and so present a completely biased picture of the opinions expressed. Over the years, many voices have been raised against the metric system, some of them by famous men. In virtually all cases, however, their opposition was based upon the expected hostility of the ordinary citizen to any tampering with his familiar weights and measures; there has been a singular absence of evidence from anyone who had actually used the metric system and found it unsatisfactory.

A solitary quotation must suffice here; it is from the Report of the Hodgson Committee, reporting to Parliament in 1951:

'Bearing all these arguments in mind, we have come to the unanimous conclusion that the metric system is, in the broadest sense and in the interests of world uniformity, a "better" system of weights and measures than the imperial; that a change from imperial to metric for all trade purposes is sooner or later inevitable; that a continuation of the present option to use either the metric or imperial until the inevitable comes about will cause in the long run more inconvenience than an ordered change within a specified period; and that the long-term advantages which would flow from an organised change in the near future would far outweigh the inconveniences of the change itself' [5].

The metric system has been in existence for nearly two centuries now, and in all that has been written about it throughout this time there is never anything approaching a serious expression of dissatisfaction by someone who has had occasion to use it sufficiently to become familiar with it; still less an unfavourable comparison with the imperial system. The tide of opinion has flowed consistently the other way, and has been opposed only by arguments relating to the cost and inconvenience of change.

Science and art belong to the whole world, and the
barriers of nationality vanish before them.
Goethe

4
Advantages in Specialised Use

When we turn to the highly sophisticated calculations of science
and technology we find that the scene is quite different. The use of
fractions has virtually disappeared; almost all calculations are made in
decimals. The occurrence of very large or very small numbers is no longer
regarded as undesirable, so that the sizes of units are less important, and
calculations are frequently carried right through in terms of a single unit
for each quantity. A variety of completely new units appear, in addition
to the familiar 'weights and measures' which suffice for most domestic
and commercial purposes. It will accordingly be impossible to avoid
technicalities in the following discussion.

Most engineers in this country use a selection of units drawn from the
imperial system, together with certain metric units in areas such as electro-
technology where imperial units have not been developed. A small minority
engaged in branches of industry with strong continental connections use
the 'metric technical' system, the continental engineers' version of the
metric system. Most scientists use the metric system exclusively, though
not all make the same selection of metric units.

4.1 Alternative units
It is in this area that the distinction between the conventional metric
system and the International System ('SI') becomes all-important. The
ideas underlying the development of SI have already been briefly mentioned, but they must now be examined more closely. We start by returning
to a simple type of calculation already encountered more than once in

earlier sections; determining the cost of a given quantity when the price of unit quantity is known. The principle underlying the calculation may be written in the form of an equation:

$$(\text{price}) = (\text{quantity}) \times (\text{cost per unit quantity})$$

and the essential arithmetic is just a single multiplication. Suppose we wished to find the cost of 7 yards of ribbon at 6p a yard; we might say it is 'obviously' $7 \times 6 = 42$p, but in fact we are doing something a little more complicated than that; when written out in full the calculation appears as

$$7 \text{ yd} \times \frac{6p}{yd},$$

and in obtaining the answer we are not only multiplying 7 by 6 but cancelling out the yard units as well. It is to be observed that the full equation representing this numerical example is an exact parallel to the basic relation given earlier:

$$(42p) = (7 \text{ yd}) \times \left(\frac{6p}{yd}\right).$$

Suppose, however, that we had been asked to work out the cost of 7 yards at 2p per foot. The same basic principles would lead to

$$7 \text{ yd} \times \frac{2p}{ft},$$

but we know that 7×2 would give the wrong answer, and the reason is clear; we cannot cancel out a yard against a foot. To obtain the right answer we must change from yards to feet, or vice versa, introducing the conversion factor 3; the full numerical equation then has an additional term:

$$(42p) = (7 \text{ yd}) \times \left[\frac{3 \text{ ft}}{yd}\right] \times \left(\frac{2p}{ft}\right).$$

The yards can now be cancelled against each other, and so can the feet, leaving the units consistent again. Note, however, that the parallel with the basic relation has been destroyed by the intrusion of the extra factor [3 ft/yd]. We use square brackets to emphasise its role of changing from one unit to another. The obvious effect is an increase in the number of arithmetical operations, but the loss of the strict correspondence between the general statement and the numerical equation is also a significant disadvantage, as will be seen later. These effects have resulted from the use of two different units for a single quantity in the same calculation; the yard and the foot have been used for length.

The imperial system, as we have seen, is full of alternative units, related by non-decimal numbers, and the consequences in simple calculations have already been fully discussed. In the kind of work considered in the present section alternatives of this elementary type are avoided as far as possible. Nevertheless, the difficulty still remains because, for some of the more complicated quantities, different units have been developed separately in various branches of technology, and have become firmly established. Conversion from one unit to another is therefore repeatedly necessary.

The following example shows this difficulty in operation. A small crane driven by an electric motor hoists a load of 300 pounds at 5 feet per second. What power has to be produced by the motor, and what is its rate of consumption of electricity? The basic principle underlying this calculation is simply

$$\text{(power)} = \text{(force)} \times \text{(speed)};$$

here the force is 300 lbf and the speed is 5 ft/s, so that we may write, as a parallel to the basic relation,

$$\left(1500 \,\frac{\text{ft lbf}}{\text{s}}\right) = (300 \text{ lbf}) \times \left(5 \,\frac{\text{ft}}{\text{s}}\right)$$

However, the unit of power which appears on the left-hand side, the ft lbf/s, is not one that has become popular; British engineers would almost certainly expect to use the horse-power, which equals 550 ft lbf/s, so the answer must be divided by 550 to make it acceptable. Since $1500 \div 550 = 2.73$, the numerical equation appears as follows:

$$(2.73 \text{ hp}) = (300 \text{ lbf}) \times \left(5 \,\frac{\text{ft}}{\text{s}}\right) \times \left[\frac{\text{hp}}{550 \text{ ft lbf/s}}\right]$$

which is consistent as regards units but is no longer in the same form as the basic relation. To determine the rate of consumption of electricity we should not really need any further calculation, since this is still just a matter of the power required (for simplicity, we are ignoring the losses in the motor itself); it would in fact be quite correct to give the same answer, namely 2.73 hp; but this unit is, by convention, not used for electricity, and a further conversion is needed to make the answer intelligible. The appropriate unit is the kilowatt, and since 1 hp = 0.746 kW and $2.73 \times 0.746 = 2.03$, we obtain a still more complicated numerical equation:

$$(2.03 \text{ kW}) = (300 \text{ lbf}) \times \left(5 \frac{\text{ft}}{\text{s}}\right) \times \left[\frac{\text{hp}}{550 \text{ ft lbf/s}}\right] \times \left[\frac{0.746 \text{ kW}}{\text{hp}}\right]$$

This has departed even further from the basic relation, and instead of the single multiplication which should have been sufficient there are two more operations—division by 550 and multiplication by 0.746.

We are perhaps not surprised to find this sort of thing in the imperial system, but in fact a similar calculation in the conventional metric system produces a similar result: the simple calculation gives an answer in terms of the kgf m/s, which has to be divided by 75 to convert to metric horse-power, and then multiplied by 735.5 to give the consumption of electricity in kilowatts. Many other examples of this kind could be cited. The full range of metric units for power includes not only the three just mentioned but the kilocalorie per hour, the erg per second, and several others less often used. Alternatives are available in the same way for other important quantities. The effect, to repeat what has just been said, is two-fold: an unnecessary increase in the arithmetic, and a confusing loss of similarity between numerical equations and the relations between quantities on which they are based. The latter can be a severe handicap when carrying out unfamiliar calculations, and is particularly so for students who have not yet achieved a secure grasp of the subject.

4.2 The principle of coherence

The International System was devised to do away with this imperfection of the earlier metric system. SI contains no alternative units at all; for any quantity there is only one possible unit (it will be understood that we are not now concerned with the metric prefixes, which adjust the sizes of units by multiples of ten). Furthermore, numerical and basic equations always correspond exactly.

The concept of such a system is more subtle than might be supposed. It is not just a matter of choosing a single unit for each quantity and sticking to our decision. Suppose we decided to make a unique selection of units from the imperial system, and began by choosing the foot as unit of length. For area, we might decide to choose the acre. But consider the procedure for calculating an area: the basic relation is

$$(\text{area}) = (\text{length}) \times (\text{length})$$

and a typical numerical example might be

$$(\text{area}) = (3 \text{ ft}) \times (5 \text{ ft})$$

Evidently, if we are to retain a direct correspondence between these two, we must be able to put 15 on the left-hand side of the numerical equation, and this is only possible if the unit of area is the square foot. We are not allowed, therefore, to choose the acre as our unit; by choosing the foot for length we have already committed ourselves to the square foot for area. In the same way we must use the cubic foot for volume; we are not at liberty to choose, say, the gallon. Our freedom of choice has already been noticeably restricted, even though we have so far only chosen one unit.

Such considerations lead to the principle of 'coherence'. In order to develop a system of units which will have the properties we have been discussing, we start by defining a very small number of independent units—the so-called 'base' units. Then we construct other units by combining base units together in accordance with physical principles; these are called 'derived' units. We avoid bringing in numerical factors, and we do not introduce any more separately-defined units unless it is quite impossible to form a suitable unit from the base units so far defined. A system of units so constructed is said to be *coherent*.

4.3 The International System (SI)

The International System was developed in this manner, and is accordingly a coherent system [19]. In order that its introduction should cause the least possible disturbance to existing practice, the 'base' units were carefully chosen so that as many as possible of the units in the system should already be in use. The first four base units are the metre, kilogramme, second and ampere, which have long been firmly established. The remainder are more specialised: the kelvin, for temperature, which corresponds to the Centigrade (more correctly now the Celsius) thermometer scale, the candela for luminous intensity, and the mole for the chemists' 'amount of substance'. All other units are built up from these seven. Area becomes the square metre, or m^2; volume, the cubic metre or m^3. The physical principle underlying the concept of velocity is distance divided by time, so the SI unit is the metre per second or m/s, and similarly, acceleration is represented by the m/s^2. To obtain a unit of force we invoke the physical principle force is mass times acceleration, so that the SI unit is the (kg) $\times$ (m/s^2), or $kg\ m/s^2$. Work is force times distance moved, and the SI unit is (kg m/s^2) $\times$ (m), or $kg\ m^2/s^2$; power is rate of doing work, that is work divided by time, and the unit is the $kg\ m^2/s^3$; and so on. By using a set of units developed in this way, all numerical equations correspond precisely to the physical relations on which they are based, and extraneous conversion factors never appear.

A somewhat inconvenient consequence of this procedure is that many derived units have rather complicated names, tedious to say and write, even when abbreviated. For this reason some of the more important of the derived units have been given additional, simpler names, which are usually taken from the names of famous scientists of the past. (Many of these are British: another indication, if one is really needed, that the International System is not just a foreign system!) Thus the unit of force, the kg m/s², is called the newton, abbreviated to N; the unit of work is called the joule or J; the unit of power is the watt or W. The last-named is no different from the unit which has long been familiar as the unit of electrical power, and it is one of the most important features of the International System that the units of mechanics and of electricity are brought together for the first time.

4.4 Calculations in SI units

A few examples will now be given of typical technical calculations, since this is the only really convincing way of demonstrating the advantages of working with coherent units. The following has been taken from a paper by an American aeronautical engineer [20]. It is required to calculate the pressure produced by a sound wave of 130 decibels at an altitude of 4000 ft. The basic relation is

$$(\text{pressure}) = \sqrt{\{2\times (\text{density of air})\times(\text{velocity of sound})\times (\text{intensity of sound wave})\}}$$

and the necessary data can be obtained from any handbook of aeronautics. We find the following:

density of air at 4000 ft = 0.0024 slugs/ft³
velocity of sound in air at 4000 ft = 704 mph
intensity at 130 dB, which is equivalent to 0.001 W/cm²

All we have to do in principle is substitute these values in the equation, but it is obvious that the units are completely incompatible as they stand. There are several ways of proceeding; one way is to convert the units so that everything is expressed in terms of the foot, second, pound and pound-force. We then have

66

density, $\left(0.0024 \dfrac{\text{slugs}}{\text{ft}^3}\right) \times \left[\dfrac{32.2 \text{ lb}}{\text{slug}}\right]$

resulting in a unit of lb/ft³;

velocity, $\left(704 \dfrac{\text{mile}}{\text{hour}}\right) \times \left[\dfrac{5280 \text{ ft}}{\text{mile}}\right] \times \left[\dfrac{\text{hour}}{3600 \text{ s}}\right]$

resulting in a unit of ft/s;

intensity, $\left(0.001 \dfrac{\text{W}}{\text{cm}^2}\right) \times \left[\dfrac{\text{hp}}{746 \text{ W}}\right] \times \left[\dfrac{550 \text{ ft lbf/s}}{\text{hp}}\right] \times \left[\dfrac{30.48^2 \text{ cm}^2}{\text{ft}^2}\right]$

resulting in a unit of lbf/ft s.

Putting these into the basic relation gives the pressure as

$$\sqrt{\left\{2\times \left(0.0024 \times 32.2 \dfrac{\text{lb}}{\text{ft}^3}\right) \times \left(\dfrac{704 \times 5280}{3600} \dfrac{\text{ft}}{\text{s}}\right) \times \right.}$$
$$\left.\left(\dfrac{0.001 \times 550 \times 30.48^2}{746} \dfrac{\text{lbf}}{\text{ft s}}\right)\right\}$$

and the combined units on the right-hand side are now

$$\dfrac{\text{lb}}{\text{ft}^3} \times \dfrac{\text{ft}}{\text{s}} \times \dfrac{\text{lbf}}{\text{ft s}}$$

The unit of pressure normally used in aeronautics is the lbf/ft², and since we have to take the square root we must work towards lbf²/ft⁴ on the right-hand side. To arrange this we introduce a further conversion factor,

$$\left[\dfrac{\text{lbf}}{32.2 \text{ lb ft/s}^2}\right]$$

which has the desired effect. Assembling all the figures we have finally

$$\text{pressure} = \sqrt{\left\{2\times(0.0024\times32.2)\times \left(\dfrac{704\times5280}{3600}\right) \times \right.}$$
$$\left.\left(\dfrac{0.001\times550\times30.48^2}{746}\right) \times \left(\dfrac{1}{32.2}\right)\right\} \text{ lbf/ft}^2$$

$$= 1.84 \text{ lbf/ft}^2$$

It should be noted that the original statement involved three quantities only, together with the factor 2; we are now confronted with eight *additional* numbers, though we may be alert enough to notice that 32.2

appears twice and may be cancelled out. Quite apart from the fact that the arithmetic has been almost trebled, providing further opportunities for arithmetical error, the route towards the solution is long and tortuous, and it would have been all too easy to lose the way and commit a more serious blunder. Care and thought are needed at all stages of the calculation, reducing speed and giving rise to mental fatigue. All resemblance between the final numerical equation and the original basic relation has been completely buried beneath the load of conversion factors.

One of the primary objectives of SI is to enable us to use basic relations without modification. In this case we should have, in SI units, density, 1.236 kg/m³; velocity, 314.7 m/s; intensity, 10 kg/s³. Insertion in the basic relation gives

$$\text{pressure} = \sqrt{\left\{ 2 \times (1.236 \, \frac{kg}{m^3}) \times (314.7 \, \frac{m}{s}) \times (10 \, \frac{kg}{s^3}) \right\}}$$

The units combine to give

$$\sqrt{\left\{ \frac{kg^2}{m^2 \ s^4} \right\}} \ \text{or} \ \frac{kg \ m/s^2}{m^2}$$

which is the pascal, the SI unit of pressure, so that we merely have to carry out the multiplication without more ado:

$$\sqrt{(2 \times 1.236 \times 314.7 \times 10)} = 88.2 \, \text{Pa}$$

The reduction of the arithmetic to the absolute minimum is gratifying, but even more impressive is the greatly increased simplicity and clarity of the whole calculation. The numerical equation corresponds exactly with the basic relation. There is no need to worry about the units and check them with care; if the basic relation is correct, the answer must automatically be in the right unit.

This example was deliberately chosen to combine several different sources of alternative units, including the possibility that some of the data required for an imperial calculation may be in metric units. The following slightly simpler examples provide straightforward comparisons between imperial and SI working.

In the first, we wish to calculate the amount of heat produced by the complete conversion of a quantity of fissionable material in an atomic pile. The basic relation here is Einstein's $E = mc^2$, where E is the heat produced, m the quantity of material consumed, and c the velocity of light. In imperial units we might have (say) 1 ounce of material, and $c = 186\,000$ miles per second, and we require E to be expressed in British thermal units. The numerical equation, including the necessary unit conversions, is

$$(E) = (1 \text{ oz}) \times \left[\frac{\text{lb}}{16 \text{ oz}}\right] \times \left(186\,000 \frac{\text{mile}}{\text{s}}\right)^2 \times \left[5280 \frac{\text{ft}}{\text{mile}}\right]^2 \times$$

$$\left[\frac{\text{lbf}}{32.2 \text{ lb ft/s}^2}\right] \times \left[\frac{\text{Btu}}{778 \text{ ft lbf}}\right]$$

$$= \frac{1 \times (186\,000 \times 5280)^2}{16 \times 32.2 \times 778} \text{ Btu}$$

$$= 2.4 \times 10^{12} \text{ Btu} \ (2.4 \text{ million million Btu})$$

Note the extra arithmetic and the loss of similarity to the basic relation. Compare the working when using SI units: with m = (say) 0.03 kg, and c = 3 × 10⁸ m/s, we have

$$(E) = (0.03 \text{ kg}) \times \left(3 \times 10^8 \frac{\text{m}}{\text{s}}\right)^2$$

$$= 0.03 \times (3 \times 10^8)^2 \frac{\text{kg m}^2}{\text{s}^2}$$

$$= 2700 \times 10^{12} \text{ J}$$

$$= 2700 \text{ TJ}$$

since kg m²/s² is the SI unit for heat, also known as the joule (J). Note the absence of extraneous numbers, and the strict parallel to the basic relation. (Note also that even for such extremely large quantities the prefix language of SI provides a unit of convenient size—the terajoule.)

In this example the imperial working involved three extra numbers: 5280, to convert miles into feet; 32.2 to convert an unfamiliar unit of force into the customary lbf; and 778 to convert from a unit used only for mechanical work into a conventional heat unit. The SI working avoided all these because it admits of no alternatives and the need for conversion never arises.

The second example is to calculate the maximum power which can be transmitted by a rotating shaft. The basic relation is

$$(\text{power}) = \left(\frac{\pi}{16}\right) \times (\text{rotational speed}) \times (\text{diameter of shaft})^3 \times$$

$$(\text{maximum permissible stress})$$

and in imperial units we might have a speed of 400 rev/min, a shaft size of 3.0 in, and a maximum stress of 6000 lbf/in². We should expect to find the answer expressed as horse-power, and the full numerical equation is

$$(\text{power}) = \left(\frac{\pi}{16}\right) \times \left(400\ \frac{\text{rev}}{\text{min}}\right) \times \left[\frac{\text{min}}{60\ \text{s}}\right] \times \left[\frac{2\pi\ \text{rad}}{\text{rev}}\right] \times (3.0\ \text{in})^3 \times$$

$$\left[\frac{\text{ft}}{12\ \text{in}}\right]^3 \times \left(6000\ \frac{\text{lbf}}{\text{in}^2}\right) \times \left[\frac{12\ \text{in}}{\text{ft}}\right]^2 \times \left[\frac{\text{hp}}{550\ \text{ft lbf/s}}\right]$$

$$= 202\ \text{hp (treating the radian as unity)}$$

In SI units we might have a speed of 40 rad/s, a diameter of 76 mm or 0.076 m, and a stress of 40 MN/m² or 40×10^6 N/m²; the power is then given by

$$(\text{power}) = \left(\frac{\pi}{16}\right) \times \left(40\ \frac{\text{rad}}{\text{s}}\right) \times (0.076\ \text{m})^3 \times \left(40 \times 10^6\ \frac{\text{N}}{\text{m}^2}\right)$$

$$= 138\ 000\ \text{W or 138 kW}$$

Note once again the remarkable clarity of the SI solution, and the usual saving in arithmetic.

The third example, a very simple one, re-emphasises an important feature of SI. Suppose we have an electric generator whose output is 2 MW. Its efficiency is 85 per cent. It is driven by an engine having an efficiency of 28 per cent, using fuel with a calorific value of 17 500 Btu/lb. We wish to know the power the engine must develop and the rate of consumption of fuel.

The power supplied to the generator must be $2 \div 0.85 = 2.35$ MW, and this is accordingly the output of the engine, but to express it in the familiar horse-power we convert by means of the factor

$$\left[\frac{\text{hp}}{746\ \text{W}}\right]$$

and get 3150 hp. The power consumed by the engine must therefore be $3150 \div 0.28 = 11\ 250$ hp. To determine the fuel consumption we first change from hp to ft lbf/s by means of

$$\left[\frac{550\ \text{ft lbf/s}}{\text{hp}}\right]$$

and then to Btu/s by means of

$$\left[\frac{\text{Btu}}{778\ \text{ft lbf/s}}\right]$$

Figure 7

The Watt: Unique Unit of Power in the International System

Power = Watt (W) = J/s = N m/s = rate of doing work

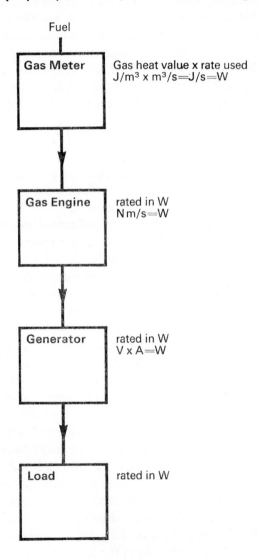

Fuel

Gas Meter — Gas heat value x rate used
J/m³ x m³/s=J/s=W

Gas Engine — rated in W
N m/s=W

Generator — rated in W
V x A=W

Load — rated in W

1 joule of work done in 1 second is 1 watt of power

obtaining $(11\ 250 \times 550) \div 778 = 7950$ Btu/s; the fuel consumption is therefore $7950/17\ 500 = 0.45$ lb/s.

In SI we follow the same route; the output of the engine is again $2 \div 0.85 = 2.35$ MW, but this can now stand without further modification because in SI all power is measured in watts. The input to the engine is therefore $2.35 \div 0.28 = 8.39$ MW. If the calorific value of the fuel is given as 40 MJ/kg, the required consumption is $8.39 \div 40 = 0.21$ kg/s.

The important point here is that this calculation has scarcely involved any interplay between one unit and another; it is simply a matter of adjusting power quantities by efficiency factors. Nevertheless, in the imperial working we have met the megawatt, horse-power, ft lbf/s, and Btu/s, together with the associated numbers 746, 550, and 778. In SI these are all represented by the same unit, the watt, or its alternative form the joule per second (*see* Figure 7, page 71).

4.5 Advantages of the International System

It is now apparent that there are three main sources of alternative units and their associated conversion factors.

1 The existence of units of different sizes for one quantity; this is effectively avoided in the metric system because of the decimal relations between such units.

2 The co-existence of units arising in different branches of technology; this is *not* avoided in the earlier versions of the metric system.

3 The intrusion of metric units into an imperial calculation, usually because scientific data are normally expressed in metric terms.

A striking indication of the magnitude of this problem is provided by the existence of a British Standard which is concerned wholly with tables provided to facilitate conversion between a number of commonly used units [21]. It has two parts and a supplement, and extends to over 500 pages in all; and it is a best-seller! A typical engineer's handbook, chosen at random, includes nearly 30 pages concerned with unit-conversion. The number of different units available for some quantities is extraordinary. A recent design manual lists the following units of pressure: lbf/in^2, $tonf/in^2$, lbf/ft^2, $tonf/ft^2$, kgf/cm^2, kgf/mm^2; inch of water, foot of water, millimetre of water; inch of mercury, millimetre of mercury; bar, torr, atmosphere. A data sheet on viscosity [22] lists no less than 40 possible units for dynamic viscosity, and gives a table showing the 56 conversion factors resulting from eight of the commonest of these units (*see* Figure 8, page 73). The same source gives a table of 56 factors linking eight units for

Conversion Factors for Dynamic Viscosity

Figure 8

1 ... =	$\dfrac{kg}{m\,s}$ or $\dfrac{N\,s}{m^2}$ (SI unit)	$\dfrac{10^{-2}\,g}{cm\,s}$ or $\dfrac{10^{-2}\,dyn\,s}{cm^2}$ (centipoise)	$\dfrac{kgf\,s}{m^2}$	$\dfrac{lb}{ft\,s}$ or $\dfrac{pdl\,s}{ft^2}$	$\dfrac{lb}{ft\,h}$	$\dfrac{pdl\,h}{ft^2}$	$\dfrac{slug}{ft\,s}$ or $\dfrac{lbf\,s}{ft^2}$	$\dfrac{lbf\,s}{in^2}$ (reyn)
1 SI unit = $1\,\dfrac{kg}{m\,s}$ = $1\,\dfrac{N\,s}{m^2}$ =	1	$\mathbf{\times 10^3}$	101.97×10^{-3}	671.97×10^{-3}	2.4191×10^3	186.66×10^{-6}	20.885×10^{-3}	145.04×10^{-6}
1 centipoise = $10^{-2}\,\dfrac{g}{cm\,s}$ = $10^{-2}\,\dfrac{dyn\,s}{cm^2}$ =	1×10^{-3}	1	101.97×10^{-6}	671.97×10^{-6}	2.4191	186.66×10^{-9}	20.885×10^{-6}	145.04×10^{-9}
$1\,\dfrac{kgf\,s}{m^2}$ =	9.8066	9.8066×10^3	1	6.5898	23.723×10^3	1.8305×10^{-3}	204.82×10^{-3}	1.4223×10^{-3}
$1\,\dfrac{lb}{ft\,s}$ = $1\,\dfrac{pdl\,s}{ft^2}$ =	1.4882	1.4882×10^3	151.75×10^{-3}	1	$\mathbf{3.6}\ \mathbf{\times 10^3}$	277.78×10^{-6}	31.081×10^{-3}	215.84×10^{-6}
$1\,\dfrac{lb}{ft\,h}$ =	413.38×10^{-6}	413.38×10^{-3}	42.153×10^{-6}	277.78×10^{-6}	1	77.160×10^{-9}	8.6336×10^{-6}	59.956×10^{-9}
$1\,\dfrac{pdl\,h}{ft^2}$ =	5.3574×10^3	5.3574×10^6	546.30	$\mathbf{3.6}\ \mathbf{\times 10^3}$	$\mathbf{12.96}\ \mathbf{\times 10^6}$	**1**	111.89	777.02×10^{-3}
$1\,\dfrac{slug}{ft\,s}$ = $1\,\dfrac{lbf\,s}{ft^2}$ =	47.880	47.880×10^3	4.8824	32.174	115.83×10^3	8.9372×10^{-3}	1	6.9444×10^{-3}
1 reyn = $1\,\dfrac{lbf\,s}{in^2}$ =	6.8948×10^3	6.8948×10^6	703.07	4.6331×10^3	16.679×10^6	1.2870	**144**	1

Exact values are printed in bold type to distinguish them from rounded values.

kinematic viscosity, together with another referring to seven further units used for special purposes. The amount of wasted effort represented by this babel of tongues is staggering. Individuals become accustomed to their own restricted selection of units, and convert from one to the other with comparatively little trouble, but as soon as they step aside from their own particular beaten track they get into difficulties and reach for their tables of conversion factors.

A further consequence, often overlooked, is that published scientific papers emanating from other countries (or even merely from a different branch of technology) may be almost unintelligible through being expressed in unfamiliar units. The scientist may either waste time wrestling with the task of unit-conversion or, what is worse, push the paper aside unread. It must be emphasised that this problem arises almost as frequently in the earlier metric system as in the imperial system. Only the International System does away with it altogether.

The special advantages claimed for the International System may be briefly summarised as follows:

1 Reduction in arithmetic, leading to a saving of time both directly and through the reduced opportunity for mistakes;
2 Increased clarity of calculations, leading to faster working and avoidance of serious error;
3 Increased accessibility of data and other information from external sources, resulting from the use of a single unit-language.

These claims can be supported by examining textbooks of design in imperial and SI units and comparing the worked examples. This can be impressive enough in subjects which make use of a considerable variety of units, but it undoubtedly underestimates the problem because the examples have been devised to stress the theoretical or procedural material which the student is trying to learn, and the irrelevant difficulties of unit-conversion are deliberately kept to a minimum by a careful choice of units. Even so, one may find page after page littered with numbers such as 144, 778, 746, 550, 33 000, 3600, 5280, 2240, resulting from the almost unavoidable inch/foot/mile, pound/ton, second/minute/hour, horse-power, British thermal unit and the rest. A textbook of thermodynamics containing a large number of worked examples, mostly quite short, was found to have an average of nearly three conversion factors per example [23]. The distribution is shown in the diagram (*see* Figure 9, page 75), and it can be seen from the large number of examples with no conversion factors at all that the author has, as usual, tried to avoid them as far as possible.

74

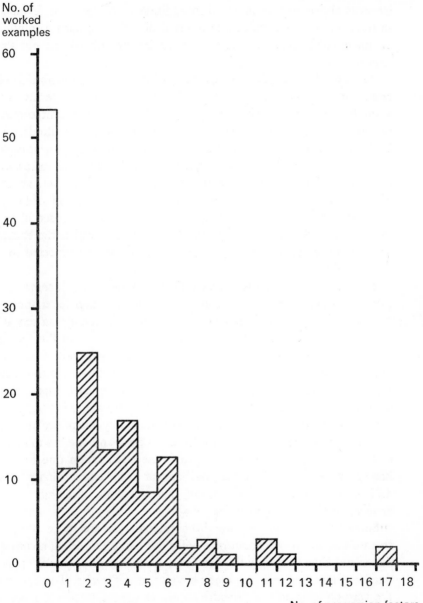

Figure 9

Number of Conversion Factors in Worked Examples in Thermodynamics

No. of worked examples

No. of conversion factors

Many textbooks include very few numerical examples, contenting themselves with so-called 'literal' solutions in which letters represent quantities and units do not appear at all. When attempting to apply such solutions to a problem expressed in imperial units a certain amount of unit-manipulation is almost always involved in addition to the arithmetic indicated in the solution. SI units can be inserted directly into such a solution, in complete confidence that the answer will be not only correct but already expressed in the required units.

Books on the design of heat exchangers afford many illustrations of the large number of different physical quantities which may be involved in a single calculation, each offering the possibility that a unit conversion may be needed. A heat exchanger will normally involve two fluids, and for each one it will be necessary to take account of the density, heat capacity, thermal conductivity and viscosity, together with the temperature and rate of flow. It will usually be required to produce information about the dimensions of the proposed heat exchanger, the rate of flow of heat, and the pressures of both fluids. Information may also be needed about the thermal and other properties of the materials from which the exchanger is to be made, and of any dirt deposits which may be expected to form upon it while in service.

We have already seen the great variety of units in which some of these calculations may be expressed, and it is quite common for a substantial proportion of the total calculation-time to be spent merely on reconciling units drawn from a variety of sources. Books on subjects of this type commonly include comprehensive sections on units and conversion factors. One oddity illustrates the perverseness of the conventions with which the use of imperial units is riddled; in heat exchanger calculations, the rate of heat-flow will be expressed in terms of the square foot and the hour, whereas pressure-drop calculations will invariably introduce the square inch and the second. Occasionally there is a clash and one has to give way, and we find (by way of example) that the acceleration due to gravity, known to everyone as 32.2 ft/s^2, may appear in the extraordinary guise of 4.17×10^8 ft/h^2. Needless to say this ridiculous situation does not arise when working in SI units.

Some of the units we have been referring to are quite complex in themselves, and if we cannot readily lay our hands on the right conversion factor and have to supply the deficiency from first principles we may find ourselves involved in a surprising amount of arithmetic. To change from the very popular unit of pressure known as the millimetre of mercury to the conventional engineer's lbf/in², we might find ourselves dividing by 25.4 to get inches and by 12 to get feet, multiplying by 13.6, the specific gravity of mercury, and by 62.3, the density of water, and finally dividing by 144. Again, to change from the commonly used centipoise, for viscosity, to the usual imperial unit requires a multiplication by $(0.01 \times 2.54 \times 12) \div 454$. Still more bizarre procedures are needed for dealing with the special units sometimes used for indicating the properties of lubricating oils. The following is a typical preliminary to the design of a journal bearing: it is assumed that the oil to be used will be of a type classified as SAE 10, and a handbook indicates that it will have a viscosity of 165 Saybolt Universal Seconds at 100 °F. To find its dynamic viscosity in centipoises we use the formula

$$\text{viscosity} = \left(0.22 \times 165 - \frac{180}{165} \right) \times \text{specific gravity,}$$

and for a calculation in imperial units we must now convert from centipoises as we have just indicated.

It is scarcely credible that designers should be going through these antics day in, day out, and in fact it is not really true. What happens is that manipulations of this kind which arise at all frequently are condensed into simple formulae or replaced by tables or charts, and the designer takes advantage of them to save himself a great deal of time. Some of these short-cut procedures can be found in handbooks; some are developed by individual designers for their own use or that of their colleagues. Frequently these formulae, etc., involve a variety of ill-assorted units, part metric, part imperial, and include numbers whose origin may be very obscure. The snag about this practice is that the designer forgets what he is really doing, or never even succeeds in understanding it; he just follows blindly the instructions provided with the formula, with the result that he gets into difficulties whenever he encounters something a little off the beaten track. This habit of producing tables and condensed formulae is so ingrained that well-intentioned efforts are now being made in some quarters to produce them in terms of SI units, overlooking the fact that the calculations they represent are utterly simple or even non-existent. It should not be thought for a moment that the proponents of SI are academic purists who want designers to do extra arithmetic just to demonstrate their grasp of the subject. SI is an essentially practical system, which has so great a simplifying effect as to render most short-cut procedures unnecessary.

77

A courageous attempt has been made to assess in monetary terms the effect which the adoption of SI might be expected to have in a big American aircraft firm [20]. The starting-point was an estimate of the proportion of an average designer's time that might be saved by the avoidance of unit-conversion and the associated difficulties. It was immediately apparent that there was a wide variation between different branches of engineering. To quote from the original report: 'The highest percentage of conversions are probably found in the fields of fluid flow and heat transfer. On the other hand, in mathematics and in non-technical work by engineers, the percentage of conversions are very low. Electronics calculations often involve a mixture of physical quantities and mathematical transformations, especially regarding communications.' It was estimated that a typical electronics engineer might spend from 20% to 25% of his time on calculations, and that about 15% to 20% of this could be saved by the adoption of SI, representing a saving of 3% to 5% of his total time. Quoting again, 'An important consideration of this approach is that the percentage refers not to the actual number of units involved in calculations, but in the time spent in using such units, including "side" calculations or retrieval of handbook information to determine the appropriate conversion factors.'

(In the light of the examples given earlier this may seem a rather conservative estimate, but it has to be remembered that unit-conversion tends to occur chiefly at the beginning and end of a calculation so that the advantage in extended calculations is reduced. On the other hand this estimate almost certainly neglects the irritation and frustration produced whenever an unfamiliar unit conversion is needed and the handbooks have to be searched, with the consequent intangible but serious effect on the efficiency of the worker. He feels instinctively that such labour is an irrelevant imposition; it is almost as though a carpenter had to find a new screwdriver every time he put in a screw.)

This kind of appraisal was applied to 14 distinct types of engineer employed by the firm. For each one, an estimate was made of the time spent on calculations, and the proportion wasted on unit-conversion; these varied from 0 to 80 minutes a day and 0% to 10% respectively (*see* Figure 10, page 79). Multiplying by the number of men employed in each category, and taking an overall average, produced an estimate of 0.4% of 'total' time wasted. This figure of course applies to very highly paid employees, and the corresponding waste of money was estimated to be about $430 000 a year.

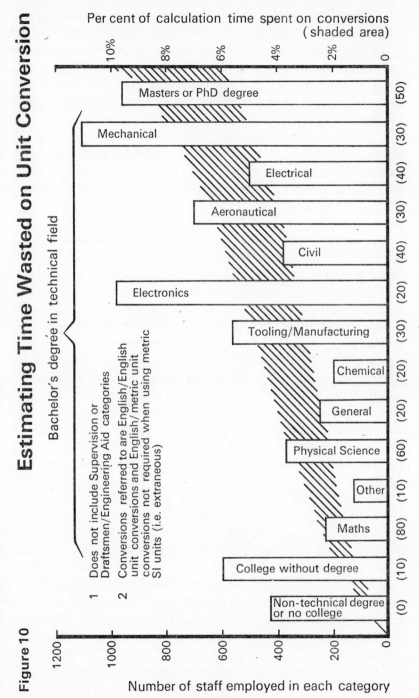

Estimating Time Wasted on Unit Conversion

Per cent of calculation time spent on conversions
(shaded area)

Masters or PhD degree

Bachelor's degree in technical field

Mechanical

Electrical

Aeronautical

Civil

Electronics

Tooling/Manufacturing

Chemical

General

Physical Science

Other

Maths

College without degree

Non-technical degree
or no college

1 Does not include Supervision or
Draftsmen/Engineering Aid categories

2 Conversions referred to are English/English
unit conversions and English/metric unit
conversions not required when using metric
SI units (i.e. extraneous)

Average calculation minutes per man-day (for each group)

Number of staff employed in each category

Figure 10

79

This analysis was limited to graduate engineers actually engaged on design, and ignored on the one hand senior staff in supervisory grades (fewer calculations, but paid more), and on the other hand draughtsmen and similar junior categories (paid less, but in much larger numbers). Including these people, on a rough-and-ready basis, raised the total sum wasted to between 0.6 and 1.0 million dollars a year, representing between 3% and 5% of the firm's net profit.

It cannot of course be pretended that this kind of analysis is very precise. Nevertheless, it at least suggests the order of magnitude of the savings which might be expected in a science-based industry from the introduction of a more sensible system of units, particularly when it is universally adopted.

4.6 SI in education

Attention has already been drawn to the increasing number of our young people who have to learn both the metric system and the imperial system. This has long been a bugbear in higher education, where many a student or sixth-former has had to face applied mathematics in imperial units, physics in cgs units, and electrical engineering in MKS units. The advantages in education of adopting a single unit-system for all subjects are obvious and indisputable. They do not, however, contribute to the present discussion about the relative merits of rival systems, except perhaps in one respect. This is the clear-cut emergence of the International System as the only one which commands a sufficient degree of international support to stand any chance at all of being accepted as the sole, unique unit-language of the future. The progressive adoption of SI into weights and measures legislation throughout the world makes the point beyond any doubt.

The solution of any technical problem requires the correct application of scientific principles and the accurate execution of the resulting arith-metic. The time-honoured method of learning by solving examples and checking the answers against the book is still as effective as any in technical subjects. The student's failure to obtain the right answer constitutes a setback, and leads him to mistrust his grasp of the principles. When this arises simply from a slip in arithmetic the effect is doubly unfortunate. Anything which reduces the possibility of error from comparatively trivial sources is a worth-while contribution to the efficiency of the learning process. It is to be hoped that the examples given earlier in this section, and the references to the numbers of conversion factors in textbook examples, will have demonstrated how much the coherent SI units have to offer in reducing arithmetic and enhancing clarity. Comparisons of solutions to examination questions, of tutorial sheets, and of reports on laboratory work, tell the same story: clearer, shorter presentation—or more in the same space. A typical examination paper in a technical subject will reveal one or more of the familiar conversion factors in almost every question; some questions may involve enough conversions to justify the allocation of a significant proportion of the marks to this alone. In almost all the questions, slips through wrong unit-conversion will lose marks, and a candidate alert enough to perceive that his answer is ridiculous may waste a disproportionate amount of time searching for his mistake. All too often he has overlooked in his haste that one dimension is in inches and the rest in feet, or has even divided by 12 when he should have multiplied, or something equally trivial.

It has long been recognised by teachers that this situation seriously impairs the effectiveness of the written examination as a means of assessment, and the improvements which follow the introduction of SI are widely welcomed for this reason.

So much trouble has been caused to students by unit problems that books have been published wholly devoted to the subject, and have achieved considerable popularity [24]. Many textbooks include substantial sections, sometimes whole chapters, on units. There is one major change introduced by SI which will probably have its greatest impact upon education, and for that reason it will be discussed here. This is the altered role of the quantity commonly known as g, the acceleration due to gravity. From an early age we are conscious of the inescapable effect of gravity; everything has weight; some things are heavier than others; we encounter the units of weight—the pound for instance; we talk of the 'force of gravity' and gradually become familiar with the concept of force, and acknowledge tacitly that weight is a force. Much later on, if our education develops a scientific bias, we become aware of a subtler concept, that of mass. If a bicycle, moving at 20 mph along a level road, hits a wall, it will scarcely leave a mark; a car moving at the same speed might cause serious damage; a heavy locomotive would probably demolish the wall completely. All three vehicles are moving on a level surface, and the force of gravity has nothing to do with the effect of their impact. The different effects result from their differing mass, or inertia. Now it so happens that the weight of a body at a given place is exactly proportional to its mass, and vice versa, so that we seldom need to bother with the distinction in non-technical matters, and we have come to use the same unit, the pound, for both purposes. As soon as we reach the level of technical education where we have to study the motion of bodies the distinction becomes very important, and the use of the same unit (or, more correctly, the use of the same name for two different units) becomes a source of confusion, and constitutes a real stumbling-block for students. In recent years, help has been provided by the introduction of a modified nomenclature; the pound is reserved for the unit of mass, and is abbreviated to lb as usual; the pound as a unit of force is called the pound-force, with the new symbol lbf. According to this convention, we say that an object having a mass of 1 lb has a weight of 1 lbf.

A physical principle relating force and mass is Newton's second law of motion: (force) = (mass) × (acceleration). Now weight is a force, and the effect of a weight of 1 lbf acting on a mass of 1 lb (ie the effect of gravity on an unsupported body) is to cause it to fall with an acceleration of about 32 ft/s². For this situation, therefore, the numerical equation corresponding to the basic relation has, on its right-hand side, (1 lb) × (32 ft/s²), but in imperial units we expect to see 1 lbf on the left-hand side. The full numerical equation must therefore include an extra factor:

$$(1 \text{ lbf}) = (1 \text{ lb}) \times (32 \text{ ft/s}^2) \times \left[\frac{\text{lbf}}{32 \text{ lb ft/s}^2} \right]$$

and the parallel with the basic relation has been destroyed. The reciprocal of the new factor

$$\left[\frac{32 \text{ lb ft/s}^2}{\text{lbf}} \right]$$

is numerically equal to the acceleration of free fall, 32 ft/s², and has accordingly been known from the earliest times as g for gravity. Once again, in recent years the attempt has been made to reduce the confusion by a changed nomenclature. The symbol g has been retained for the actual acceleration of free fall. This varies by about $\frac{1}{2}$ per cent from place to place on the earth's surface. In teaching, a new symbol g_c (or sometimes g_o) has been introduced to represent the conversion factor, and since both the lb and lbf have been given fixed values it follows that g_c also is fixed; the accurate value is

$$\left[32.1740 \, \frac{\text{lb ft/s}^2}{\text{lbf}} \right]$$

82

The effect of this 'lb, lbf, g_c' system can be seen in the following example. A mass of 10 lb moving at 8 ft/s is brought to rest by the application of a steady force over a distance of 2 ft. What is the magnitude of the force? The physical principle here is represented by the basic relation:

$$\text{(force)} = \tfrac{1}{2} \times \frac{\text{(mass)} \times \text{(velocity)}^2}{\text{(distance)}}$$

which becomes

$$\tfrac{1}{2} \times \frac{(10 \text{ lb}) \times (8 \text{ ft/s})^2}{(2 \text{ ft})}, \text{ ie } 160 \frac{\text{lb ft}}{\text{s}^2}$$

but this must be multiplied by

$$\left[\frac{\text{lbf}}{32 \text{ lb ft/s}^2} \right]$$

to obtain the required lbf unit, ie by $1/g_c$. The engineer usually short-cuts this process by boldly writing the basic relation in the modified form:

$$\text{(force)} = \tfrac{1}{2} \times \frac{\text{(mass)} \times \text{(velocity)}^2}{g_c \times \text{(distance)}}$$

This gives no trouble to the experienced man who has used it for years, but it is a constant source of confusion to the student. He not unnaturally identifies the g_c with gravity, and is worried because in so many applications the problem has nothing to do with gravity at all. He sometimes explores the unit relations on the assumption that g_c is really 32 ft/s²; leaving out the numbers, this gives on the right-hand side

$$\frac{\text{lb (ft/s)}^2}{\text{(ft/s}^2) \text{ ft}} = \text{lb}$$

which consoles him until he remembers that he has been taught that a force is to be expressed in lbf, not lb. Quite often he gives up trying to understand and endeavours to learn the formulae by rote. This inevitably results in errors, through putting g in the numerator instead of the denominator, or forgetting it altogether, or putting it blindly into other formulae where it does not belong. This 'g trouble' is almost a joke among students, though the humour must seem misplaced to some of them.

It has already been explained that the International System forms its unit of force, the newton, coherently from the metre, kilogramme, and second. The g difficulty therefore disappears, and the above calculation

83

takes the following form: A mass of 10 kg moving at 8 m/s is brought to rest in 2 m. What is the force? Putting the numbers into the basic relation gives

$$(\text{force}) = \tfrac{1}{2} \times \frac{(10 \text{ kg}) \times (8 \text{ m/s})^2}{(2 \text{ m})}$$

$$= 160 \frac{\text{kg m}}{\text{s}^2}$$

and since the kg m/s^2 is the same as the newton the calculation is at an end. The arithmetic as usual is slightly reduced, but far more important is the disappearance of the baffling g.

There is a price to pay for this improvement. Those branches of engineering which are concerned almost exclusively with problems involving gravitational forces, eg the design of a floor to support the weight of the people standing on it, have in the past benefited from the use of the gravitational unit of force. The basis of such a calculation is data about the strength of the materials to be used in the structure, and this will be expressed in terms of the lbf. When it comes to finding the weight supported by the floor, it is possible to say without any calculation at all that 1 lb weighs 1 lbf, and the work can proceed at once.

In SI, strength-of-materials data are expressed in terms of the newton, and it is therefore necessary to find out the weight in newtons of a body whose mass is given in kilogrammes. Once again we use Newton's law. We know that, unsupported, the body would fall with acceleration g; this is the effect upon it of the force known as its weight; it follows that (weight) = (mass) $\times$ (g). Here g is the acceleration of free fall in terms of the metre and second, and has the value 9.81 m/s^2 approximately. With the mass expressed in kilogrammes the combined unit is kg m/s^2, ie the newton, so that we have finally the simple rule that the weight of a body of mass 1 kg is 9.81 N approximately. The structural engineer contemplating a load of, say, 2000 kg will have to start by converting it to 2000 $\times$ 9.81 N, so that as far as he is concerned g effectively now appears where formerly it was absent. This is not as serious a matter as might be supposed, since g is now directly and obviously associated with the force of gravity, and its presence is far less likely to confuse. Fundamentally, there is a big advantage; the value of g which must be used is now the true, local value, and though it varies very little on earth, the formulae in which it appears are just as applicable to extra-terrestrial conditions, for example, on the moon. With our present system we have to face the confusing situation that a pound of rock does not weigh a pound on the moon.

It is fortuitous that the numerical value of g on earth in m/s^2 is only 2 per cent less than 10, so that a very simple calculation is possible if this degree of inaccuracy can be tolerated.

The same situation of confusion about g exists in the present engineers' version of the metric system, with the kg as the unit of mass and the kgf as the unit of force. The kilogramme-force is gradually being phased out, although it is still extensively used.

4.7 Miscellaneous comments on the International System

Much of the previous discussion in this section has been concerned with the superiority of the International System over the imperial system. Since virtually all scientific work is now carried out in the metric system, it is desirable to include a brief discussion of the distinctions between 'International' and 'metric'. SI is a branch of the metric system and all SI units are metric units, but the converse is not true; many of the familiar units of the old metric system are not part of SI, and will gradually disappear.

The replacement of the kilogramme-force by the newton has already been discussed. The kgf is, however, primarily an engineers' unit, and was introduced comparatively recently; scientists have preferred the dyne, which is similar in character to the newton but much smaller. It is in fact a member of the cgs system, which was referred to in the introduction; a system built up rather on the lines of the International System, but based on the centimetre and gramme instead of the metre and kilogramme. There are cgs counterparts to many SI units, differing only by factors of ten: the erg for energy, the poise and stokes for dynamic and kinematic viscosity, the dyne per square centimetre for pressure, and a variety of electrical units. These could almost be regarded as belonging to the International System, and are likely to survive for a considerable time, but the disadvantage of retaining them indefinitely is the effort of memory involved in relating them to the proper SI units and the consequent impediment to the rapid exchange of information. The same may be said of other scientific units such as the Ångström, and the 'micron', which have been developed for special purposes and give rise to difficulties to those unfamiliar with them. The 'micron' is in fact identical with the micrometre, and the significance of the change of name is simply that the new name speaks for itself and does not have to be specially learned and remembered.

There are, in addition, certain cgs units which are not simply related to SI units, foremost among them being the calorie. This is a unit of heat based on the amount of heat required to raise the temperature of one gramme of water by one degree centigrade (now Celsius), and because this amount depends upon the temperature of the water a variety of definitions have emerged and have caused difficulties in accurate work. The SI unit, the joule, avoids this trouble. It has additionally the very great advantage of being closely linked with other important units; alternative names for it include the newton-metre and the watt-second.

The torr, a unit of pressure much used in vacuum work, is also excluded from the SI family; it is unrelated to other units and causes difficulties when introduced into calculations. The appropriate SI unit is the N/m^2, which equals 0.0075 torr, a more convenient size for many purposes.

It is worth repeating that, in the world of science, SI is the only 'live' system, in the sense that all the work on improving the definitions of units and so on is now focused on the International System. Figure 11 (page 87) shows, by way of example, the successive improvements to the precision of the metre; this is now approaching one in a thousand million. All this work is co-ordinated by the International Bureau of Weights and Measures, with headquarters near Paris. The Bureau is supervised by an International Committee, which comes under the authority of the General Conference of Weights and Measures (CGPM). The CGPM consists of delegates from all the Member States of the Metric Convention and meets at least once every six years. It was the CGPM that formally established the International System [19].

The fact that SI is noticeably different from the earlier metric system has aroused apprehension in some quarters that it will 'invade' the domestic scene and give rise to serious difficulties. For example, the strict SI units for area and volume are the square metre and cubic metre; the hectare and litre are not true SI units, and it is therefore feared that they will one day be banned, with most unfortunate consequences. Some people go further and assert that we shall have to buy potatoes by the newton, and speak of yesterday's temperature as 293 K. These alarmist reports are completely without foundation. The refinements of SI are intended for specialist use only. Nevertheless the link between the everyday form of the metric system and SI is a strong and simple one. The litre is one-thousandth of a cubic metre, or a cubic decimetre; the hectare is ten thousand square metres, or a square hectometre. Conversion is just a matter of multiplying or dividing by tens, and involves no real arithmetic.

Figure 11

Definition of the Metre
– Successive Improvements
in Precision

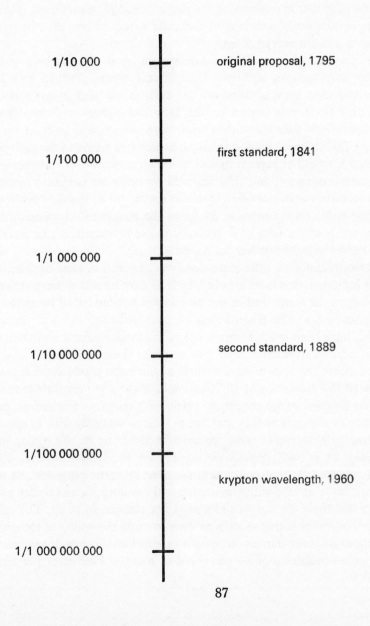

1/10 000 — original proposal, 1795

1/100 000 — first standard, 1841

1/1 000 000 —

1/10 000 000 — second standard, 1889

1/100 000 000 —

krypton wavelength, 1960

1/1 000 000 000 —

Another canard is the impression now current in some quarters that the very useful centimetre will be banned, or at least discouraged. This again is a misunderstanding of an agreement which was intended to apply to specialist use only. Engineers normally use a single unit for length, and it would be rather a pity if, for lack of any guidance, some chose to use the centimetre and others the millimetre. It has, therefore, been agreed internationally that in engineering the millimetre shall be preferred. There are one or two other decisions of a similar nature. They have little or nothing to do with everyday use.

The differences between the metric system, as it will continue to be used by most people, and the International System, which will be increasingly used by specialists, are not such as will lead to any serious difficulties. Their only impact on the man-in-the-street will arise from his comparatively rare encounters with more complicated units. A tyre-pressure, for instance, quoted in imperial units in terms of pounds per square inch, would at present appear in a metric country in kilogrammes per square centimetre, and this unit will probably be familiar to many British motorists who have taken their cars abroad; in SI it will be replaced by a unit based on the newton. As far as the motorist is concerned, the precise nature of the unit he is expected to use is immaterial; he merely has to know the right number for his car.

It is worth looking a little more closely at the units of time because, as already indicated, this is an area in which SI may be said to have arrived too late upon the scene, and in any case we are circumscribed by astronomical phenomena. The sole SI unit of time is the second, and though scientists have been quick to make use of the usual prefixes, and refer to milliseconds, microseconds, and nanoseconds, these are matters which do not concern the man-in-the-street. If a calculation produces an answer such as 10.75 kiloseconds or 10 750 seconds it conveys very little to most of us. As long as we are concerned solely with technical matters we can leave such expressions as they are; but as soon as we really wish to appreciate how long a process takes we have to divide by 60, 60 again, and sometimes 24 as well, before we achieve an intelligible answer. The second is indeed far too small a unit for most domestic purposes and we are much more at ease with the minute and the hour. For everyday use, the fact that these are not SI units need not concern us at all. The only point to remember is that as soon as we move into the region of technical calculations we must convert our measurements into seconds. It may seem much more sensible to quote the speed of a car in kilometres per hour than in metres per second, since we can so easily work out the distance travelled in a quarter of an hour, or the time needed to cover 100 km; and there is no reason whatever to change this practice. Nevertheless, as soon as we try to calculate, say, a braking distance, we find ourselves converting 40 km/h into $40\,000 \div 3600$ m/s, thereby introducing just the kind of unit-conversion that SI was intended to avoid. The second, therefore, should be preferred whenever it has no obvious disadvantages, and certainly for all technical work.

It will be advantageous to apply the same philosophy generally. We should consider very carefully, before adopting any departure from the strict principles of SI, whether the apparent advantages of greater familiarity or convenience are sufficiently real to offset the disadvantages which will certainly arise as soon as one moves into the technical sphere and encounters the interaction of one unit with another.

5
Conclusion

A system of units is a branch or extension of language; it enables us to communicate with each other in precise, numerical terms. It does more than that, however, for it enormously simplifies our efforts to think and reason about quantitative matters (that, after all, is what calculating really means). In the course of this survey we have examined the metric system from both points of view, over the whole range of human activity. It is, no doubt, not a perfect system; nevertheless, in virtually all its aspects it seems to be superior to any alternative available to us at the present time. Sometimes its advantages are substantial, sometimes only marginal, but scarcely ever does it prove inferior. In its latest form, the International System, it is undoubtedly the best we are likely to be offered for a very long time to come.

We learn about weights and measures at a very early age, when our ability to absorb new knowledge is at its greatest. It is impossible for us to assess objectively, in our maturity, the merits of an entirely new system. It can never become, try as we may, as much 'second nature' as the one we learned at school, and it may be a very long time before its inherent advantages outweigh its unfamiliarity. Surely, however, we can be discerning enough to acknowledge the inevitable bias in our judgement of these matters, and can strive to examine dispassionately the evidence before us, and listen to the testimony of those who have really immersed themselves in the metric system. Among all the voices that ask to be heard, those of people concerned with the education of the young should perhaps command our most careful attention. Not for nothing do teachers write of a 'SI of relief' [25].

References

1 Skinner, F G (1967) Weights and Measures: a Science Museum Survey. HMSO.
2 The New English Bible (1970) Oxford, Cambridge University Presses.
3 Breed, W R (1964) The Weights and Measures Act, 1963. Chas. Knight & Co.
4 NASA Publications Manual SP 7013 (1964).
5 Report of the Committee on Weights and Measures Legislation (Hodgson Committee) (1951) Cmd 8219. HMSO.
6 Mechanical Engineering (1965) **87**, March, p. 89.
7 *A Metric America: A decision whose time has come.* Superintendent of Documents, US Government Printing Office, Washington DC. July 1971.
8 Hansard (1907) 171, col. 1358. HMSO.
9 Report of the Select Committee on Weights and Measures (1862) House of Commons.
10 Hough, F W (1960) Why adopt the metric system ? *Civil Engineering*, New York, 30, November, p. 73.
11 Metrication in Secondary Education (1969) The Royal Society.
12 Joint Report of Committees appointed by the British Association and the Association of British Chambers of Commerce 'Decimal Coinage and the Metric System. Should Britain Change ?' (1960). Butterworth.
13 Report of the (Australian) Senate Select Committee on the Metric System of Weights and Measures (1968) Canberra: Parliamentary Paper 19.

91

14 Walmsley, R M (1894) Transactions, Royal Scottish Society of Arts, pp. 445-461.

15 Report from Her Majesty's Representatives in Europe (and abroad) on the metric system (1900) Part I, Cd 253, XC 199; (1901) Part II, Cd 435, LXXX 1023.

16 Report of the Select Committee on Weights and Measures (Metric System) Bill (1904).

17 Cited in Hallock, W & Wade, H T (1906) The Evolution of Weights and Measures and the Metric System. New York: MacMillan.

18 Mechanical Engineering (1965) **87**, Jan., May.

19 BS 3763: 1970 The International System of Units (SI) British Standards Institution.

20 Henning, G E (1966) Metric metrology in aerospace engineering. Society of Aeronautical Weight Engineers Inc. Technical Paper No. 526.

21 BS 350: Conversion Factors and Tables. (1959) Part 1, Basis of Tables; Conversion Factors. (1962) Part 2, Detailed Conversion Tables. (1967) Supplement No. 1, Additional Tables for SI Conversions. British Standards Institution.

22 Engineering Sciences Data Item No. 68036, Introductory Memorandum on the viscosity of liquids and the classification of lubricating oils (1968) Institution of Mechanical Engineers.

23 Boxer, G (1966) Examples in Engineering Thermodynamics. Edward Arnold.

24 Walshaw, A C (1954, 1964, 1967) Engineering Units and Worked Examples. Blackie & Son Ltd.

25 Jardine, J (1965) Physics is Fun. Heinemann Educational Books Ltd.

Printed in England for Her Majesty's Stationery Office by Headley Brothers Ltd 109 Kingsway London WC2B 6PX and Ashford Kent   Dd 503723 K80 10/72

£1·25
wm8